THE RULES handbook

"There is a certain kind of woman who is given to long tousled hair, sheer black pantyhose, and acting maddeningly elusive to every man . . . She is breezy, confident, and independent, as well as coy, manipulative, and very, very hard to get. She is a Rules Girl."

—*New York Times*

" . . . We're not talking about a business deal here, but getting the man you want to propose and then to turn that proposal into an actual wedding date—it's a feat some women would say can be tougher than any corporate transaction. Of course, it's made much easier by doing *The Rules*."

—*Complete Woman*

"If you're a single woman trying to keep your own life from becoming a soap opera, then *The Rules* has something to tell you."

—*New Jersey Monthly*

"Waiting around is certainly not what Ellen Fein and Sherrie Schneider have in mind. Their message is clear: It's to the battlefields. Arm yourself and become a full-time Rules Girl! Practice them! Memorize the book! Make him pursue you until you catch him! And live life happily ever after. Amen."

—*Detroit News*

"Empowering . . . *The Rules* books can give you control over your dating life."

—*Mademoiselle*

"A must-read for women seeking success in romance."

—*People*

"*The Rules* is not just a book, it's a movement."

—*TIME*

"One of the best self-help books of all time."

—*Elle*

"[*The Rules*] has worked for me."

—*Beyonce (Us Weekly)*

"*The Rules* isn't just a book; it's a movement, honey!"

—Oprah

"I love *Not Your Mother's Rules*. Because of all the new
technology, I have to say I think women do give themselves
too easily to men."

—Wendy Williams

" . . . I fully admit to loving that book *The Rules*—that's my
handbook on how I got married."

—Kimora Lee Simmons

"Don't ever call! If he's interested, he'll call . . . I just finished
reading *The Rules*. That is the best book ever."

—Kelly Rowland

"*The Rules* is wonderful, but don't put that in the interview.
I don't want guys to know what we're doing!"

—Michelle Williams (*CosmoGIRL!*)

"*The Rules* is a fantastic book. I saw it online and I had to get
it. It was something I taught to my daughters and talked
to my girlfriends about. Women ought to be women. We
should embrace the mystique of being a woman [instead of]
deciding we are going to be the aggressors."

—Goldie Taylor

"For most of my life, I was not a Rules Girl. If a guy called, I
called right back. There was no intrigue. Then, about 10 years
ago (in 1995), I read the book and it became my bible."

—Cheryl Tiegs

"There is one thing about *The Rules* philosophy . . . it all boils
down to the fact that you have to play hard to get. You have
to treat yourself with self-respect and establish a little bit of
distance, so the guy has to step up to the plate and act right.
If things are not going the way they should in a relationship,
step back a little."

—Mira Sorvino (*Redbook*)

THE RULES
handbook

ELLEN FEIN &
SHERRIE SCHNEIDER

A GUIDE TO
CREATING LOVING AND
LASTING RELATIONSHIPS

DeVorss Publications
CAMARILLO CALIFORNIA

The Rules Handbook
Copyright © 2023
by Ellen Fein and Sherrie Schneider

ISBN Print Edition: 978-087516-935-4
ISBN Ebook Edition: 978-087516-936-1

Library of Congress Control Number: 2023936326

First DeVorss Publications Edition, 2023

Printed in The United States of America
DeVorss & Company, Publishers
PO Box 1389
Camarillo CA 93011-1389
www.devorss.com

Names: Fein, Ellen, author and Schneider, Sherrie, author.
Title: The rules handbook / by Ellen Fein and Sherrie Schneider
Description: First DeVorss Publications edition. | Camarillo, California: DeVorss Publications, 2023. | Summary:
"The Rules Handbook was written out of necessity. New York Times #1 bestselling authors Ellen Fein and Sherrie Schneider were hearing from readers who had successfully applied the original Rules formula but experienced frustration when dealing with others. They wanted a similar strategy to create loving and lasting relationships outside of romance as well. The Rules Handbook will help to attract the right people into your life and prevent or minimize any unnecessary hurt or disrespect. This new book is organized to help you focus on your own life first, remain happy and busy, and nurture your Higher Self, as opposed to your Lower Self. You can then set healthy boundaries with confidence, and not lose your power to distance yourself from opinions or comments others make in person or on social media. The Rules Handbook will empower you to gracefully step away from difficult people and instead, invest all that time and energy on yourself and the ones who truly love and respect you."—Provided by publisher.

Identifiers: LCCN 2023936326 (print) | LCCN 2023936327 (ebook) | ISBN 9780875169354 (trade paperback) | ISBN 9780875169361 (ebook) Subjects: LCSH: Family and Relationships. | Marriage and Long-Term Relationships. | Self-Help. | Personal Growth Self-Esteem.
Classification: LCC HQ1-2044 (print) | LCC HQ1-2044 (ebook) | DDC MDS 306.85/eng/20230912
LC record available at https://lccn.loc.gov/2023936326
LC ebook record available at https://lccn.loc.gov/2023936327

ACKNOWLEDGMENTS

We would like to thank our wonderful husbands who were always supportive and understanding while we were writing *The Rules Handbook* and while we were juggling phone consultations that sometimes interrupted family dinners and vacations! Thanks to our absolutely fantastic kids, who always gave us their take on the latest dating trends and social media, as well as family and friends who freely shared their time and dating stories.

Special thanks to our Certified Rules Dating Coaches around the world, fabulous clients, and loyal fans who encouraged us to write another book about our rules for dating, marriage, and everyone else in their lives, including parents, in-laws, siblings, friends, children, bosses, and coworkers . . . proving that you can do *The Rules* with anyone!

And a drumroll please . . . our sincere gratitude to our visionary publisher, Gary Peattie at DeVorss & Company; our agent, Danielle Seadia; and our brilliant editor, Marta M. Mobley, who gave us wonderful direction and guidance and without whom *The Rules Handbook* would have remained an idea instead of a reality.

contents

COURSE 2

NAVIGATING
NEW RELATIONSHIPS

COURSE 3

EMPOWERED DATING
~ 123

COURSE 4

EFFECTIVE COMMITMENT AND COMMUNICATION

~ 187

COURSE 5

CREATE RESPECTFUL MARRIAGES AND PARTNERSHIPS

~ 255

COURSE 6

THE RULES REFRESHER COURSE
~ 339

WEEK ONE:
Reminders Before You Jump Back into *The Rules* ~ 341

WEEK TWO:
Relationship Reminders ~ 346

THE
RULES
handbook

foreword

WHILE THE WORLD HAS CHANGED . . . HUMAN BIOLOGY HAS NOT

When we published *The Rules* in 1995, we thought we had covered it all. In no uncertain terms, we advised women that the secret to catching Mr. Right was being mysterious and playing hard to get, as women were falsely being told that they could successfully pursue men. We wrote it in a dos and don'ts style: Don't talk to a man first, don't call him, don't ask him out, don't date a married man, and so on.

The Rules became a bestselling book and women deluged us with more questions: What about long-distance? How do you get an ex back? What about managing second marriages, same-sex relationships, children, bosses, coworkers, and clients? So we wrote *The Rules II* for special situations. Then women wrote to say that, thanks to *The Rules* and *The Rules II*, they were getting engaged and married. Then our clients wanted to know how to get along with their husbands, so we wrote *The Rules for Marriage*.

In 2001, internet dating took off and women didn't know how to date in cyberspace, so we wrote *The Rules for Online Dating*. A decade later, women were sold about not calling men but weren't sure what to do about texting, Facebook,

Instagram, and other social media. So, we wrote *Not Your Mother's Rule*s for the younger generation and anyone dating with new technology.

The Rules are similar to the traditional advice mothers and grandmothers have handed down from generation to generation, but with a modern twist. Women are no longer housewives, but CEOs, MBAs, lawyers, doctors, TV anchors, and social media influencers. As we've become more aggressive in our careers, we've been told to be more aggressive with men, but it's not effective. That's why we wrote *The Rules*, to share the truth about dating.

The reality is that dating as we know it did not really exist before the eighteenth century because most families arranged marriages. In the 1700s, children were expected to choose a partner who would benefit the family. During those days, dating happened with a chaperone. Skipping to the early 1920s, young adults became more independent from their parents, and they were free to go out without a chaperone and date multiple people. After World War II, wise mothers stepped back and advised their children to take their time and get to know each other better, but throughout history, men almost always paid for everything.

You might feel that dating today is different. Maybe you were in diapers when the first *Rules* book was published in 1995! We know no one uses an answering machine anymore. Everything is texting and TikTok now. While it's true that technology and the way people meet have changed, human nature and biology have not! It doesn't matter how young or old you are, what country you live in, what you do for a living, or whether you are short or tall, brunette or blond: *The Rules* are ageless and timeless and always work because they are based on biology, not technology or trends.

introduction

Similar to our other five books, *The Rules Handbook* was born of necessity. Many of our clients who applied our original *Rules* formula to finding their lifelong partner shared their frustrations with dealing with other people in their lives, such as family, friends, romantic or marriage partners, coworkers, bosses, clients, neighbors, and acquaintances. They wanted a similar strategy to "win" over or succeed with other people. We quickly realized that they could apply *The Rules* not only to their romantic partners and husbands but to everyone in order to communicate more effectively, get along with them, and avoid getting hurt.

How *The Rules* all started! During the Wild West of dating in the early 1990s, Ellen and Sherrie met in New York City and became BFFs with a mutual interest in men, diet, and exercise, much like the women in *Sex and the City* before the television show ever existed. Sherrie shared with Ellen how she was struggling to find her dream husband. Ellen, who was married, offered some advice she had learned from a popular girl in high school. Thanks to this original set of dating instructions that would become *The Rules*, Sherrie got engaged and all their friends called them night and day for dating advice.

They decided to write all *The Rules* down to help their
friends and friends of friends, and so that there would be
no confusion as to how to properly and precisely catch Mr.
Right. Shortly thereafter, *The Rules* book was published in
1995, and they were invited to appear on a British TV talk
show. On their way back to New York at Heathrow Airport
in London, they couldn't help but notice that every British
tabloid had *The Rules* on its cover. British TV anchor Julia
Carling had sent Princess Diana a copy of *The Rules* book
for her birthday on July 1, 1996 and circled the chapter,
Don't Date a Married Man, as it was alleged the Princess was
involved with her rugby player husband, Will. The story
appeared on *Page Six* of the *New York Post*, igniting worldwide
curiosity about *The Rules*. The book became a bestseller and
Oprah and every media outlet called, thus beginning their
long and passionate journey teaching millions of women
around the world how *The Rules* really work!

Over the last twenty-five years, Ellen and Sherrie have
discovered *The Rules* not only work for romantic relationships,
but for others. If you suffer when a significant other rejects or
disappoints you or when a family member, friend, coworker
or boss doesn't acknowledge, appreciate, or give you as much
as you give them, then this book is for you! If you obsess
about every relationship ("I can't believe I took her out to
an expensive dinner for her birthday and she only bought
me drinks for mine!") or are paranoid that your coworker is
sabotaging you ("She showed my boss something I wrote on
Facebook to get me fired!") or think your in-laws hate you
("They always meddle in our marriage!"), this book is for you.
If you feel that your young or adult children are disrespecting

you and are ungrateful ("After all I've done for them!"), then this book is for you. If you feel that your clients or customers are always taking advantage of you ("They never pay on time, haggle over prices, and expect constant discounts and freebies!"), then this book is for you! And like the original *Rules* book, if you are looking for a committed love relationship or marriage ("I can't find anyone out there to date who has the same goals as me."), then this book is for you also!

The Rules Handbook is for anyone who wants to become more empowered and set clear boundaries so they no longer have to suffer from other people's behaviors or the way they treat or mistreat you. When you study *The Rules Handbook* Weekly Pep Talk and Daily Lessons, you will save time; feel confident and less confused; reduce your therapy bills; attract better friends; find peace, prosperity, and success; and get rid of self-pity, sadness, and bitterness.

While other books and coaches tell you to confront people and talk back to your husband, adult children, boss, coworkers, and clients or advise you to tell off and yell at your family members or even strangers ("Don't bother!"), to fight for your rights, to push and prod and force conversations at home and at work, and to be a badass, we are different and believe the opposite is much more effective. We advise you to gracefully pull back, not overreact, and be forward-thinking, which is taught in more detail in the following six courses.

We understand that modern-day women—whether twenty-two years old and graduating from college, in their thirties and getting a promotion, or forties and getting a divorce—feel that something is missing if they don't have a man. As fulfilling as their career, children, grandchildren, girlfriends, charity work, and hobbies are, it's not quite the same as sharing your life with a romantic partner. If you're reading this book, you've probably been hurt or discouraged or disappointed and are looking for a pain-free relationship plan with the right man. We sincerely believe *The Rules Handbook* can guide you through all the stages of your love life.

If you've had a successful career, bought your own condo, or thrived in every other area of your life, you may find playing hard to get and being a team player with your partner hard to swallow and even harder to integrate into a new way of dating. But it's easier than you think when you use *The Rules Handbook* as your guide on a daily basis. You can also use support groups (there are Facebook pages for Rules Girls to join), dating coaches (either of us or one of many women we have trained and certified in *The Rules*), as well as finding encouragement, helpful hints, and success stories on our Facebook and Instagram pages.

The Rules Handbook will guide you on how to attract the right people into your life and prevent or minimize getting unnecessarily hurt or offended. By following our simple rules, you will avoid relationships with people who don't truly like, love, or appreciate you. You will learn to focus on your own life, be happy and busy, and nurture your *Higher Self* that sees the truth and blessings in everything and everyone, as opposed to your *Lower Self* that becomes hurt, offended, or seeks revenge.

We believe that ONLY you have the power to change yourself, and you were never given a magic wand to change anyone else. In Course One, we share the importance of becoming the best version of yourself by choosing to empower the inner and outer parts of yourself with your *Higher Self*. In

Course Two, you will learn what to do when someone offends you and how it's best to step back and wait twenty-four hours to respond. In Course Three, you now *choose* to take time away to examine the errors in your thinking and behavior that may have caused the problem in the first place. In Course Four, you will discover how to actively seek love or approval from only others who truly love you when you are honest, mysterious, and set firm boundaries. And in Course Five, you will see how to empower your marriage or accept that you can't change another person who is complicated, difficult, or even toxic and that you need to tread lightly, keep your distance, or let them go.

When you follow *The Rules Handbook*, you are too happy and busy with your own life to speak to others first, get offended, or give unsolicited advice or criticism. You are too spiritually fulfilled to care if they criticize or slight you. You are like Teflon! You no longer care too much about what others say or think because you know it is your *Lower Self* abandoning yourself. You will now value only what you think about yourself and not care about other people's opinions of you or their comments in person or on social media. If someone is disrespectful or does not value you, you will now drop them quickly and move on . . . Next!

We are confident that if you read and follow our advice daily, *The Rules Handbook* offers you a tried and tested formula through which all your hard work is sure to result in you creating and maintaining more loving and long-lasting relationships and marriage. We are not licensed to practice psychology, and *The Rules* are not intended to replace psychological counseling. It is simply a dating philosophy based on our own experiences and those of thousands of women who have contacted and worked with us.

COURSE 1

Becoming
the Best Version
of Yourself

8 WEEKS

When we coach clients, we typically start with a one-hour childhood and dating history consultation. We get basic facts such as a client's age, profession, how and when she discovered *The Rules*, and information about her parents, their marriage, and what they taught her about dating, if anything. Then we find out how she met each of her boyfriends or husbands, what rules she followed, what rules she broke, and why she is contacting us. For example, most clients will say that their parents didn't teach them anything about dating, focusing solely on college, career, and finances. Or, they encouraged them to do whatever they wanted, call men, ask them out, or split the check. Sometimes their mothers will rationalize teaching their daughters *Rule*-breaking behavior, saying that, "Times have changed," when in reality, they just wanted a son-in-law and grandchildren. No pressure, of course. LOL!

In many cases, the relationship in question started out as following the way, according to *The Rules*. He spoke to her first at work or at a party or messaged her first on a dating app, but then she broke *Rules* by texting or talking to him for hours, seeing him too often, traveling for a week with him, or introducing him to her friends and family first or too soon. We will put her on a plan of pulling back, and in most cases, the guy will miss and pursue her. It works like magic! But in cases where the client made the first move online or off, pulling back may work temporarily, but long term he still won't commit because he didn't pick her. She's not his dream girl.

Most clients need ongoing consultations, as becoming a Rules Girl is not a once-and-done deal. It's a daily discipline of encouraging a man, who initially showed interest, to want you forever by being busy and a challenge, setting boundaries, and not losing yourself in the relationship. By doing *The Rules*, clients who would normally have pursued men by calling and texting and seeing them twenty-four seven or traveling to them, are too busy studying for their MBA, running a marathon, decluttering their closets, or donating to charity. It's amazing how much time "playing hard to get" saves!

Clients become the best version of themselves because doing *The Rules* forces one to build character. For example, it requires patience to wait for the guy to text you. It requires faith to believe if not him, someone better. It requires self-control not to grill him about the future on the first few dates or tell him your whole life story. It requires confidence to not accept a last-minute date but to hold out for courtship. As a result, dating becomes intentional and results-oriented, not accidental and haphazard. It becomes clear-cut and conscious, not vague. You are wise, laser-focused, and deliberate, not naïve, distracted, and all over the place.

Just when we thought our five books and five online courses covered everything, we've noticed that many women still lack mastery over keeping the mystery. We encourage our clients to become the best version of themselves before or while seeking out a lifelong partner. No matter how well a person follows *The Rules*, they need daily reminders and encouragement to carefully and consciously interact with others and set boundaries with confidence and self-esteem.

We offer these weekly coaching sessions to help you become your *Higher Self* with healthy thoughts and behavior and move away from *Lower Self* self-sabotaging ideas and

4 The Rules Handbook

habits. Whether you need help becoming a Creature
Unlike Any Other (CUAO), are coming to terms with a
dysfunctional childhood, or are trying to attract your dream
partner or job, this eight-week course will help you identify
and overcome self-defeating patterns, develop affirmations
to cancel out negative habits that have kept you in despair,
and learn how to improve your dating life as well as your
interactions with family, friends, and colleagues. The
information you will learn here applies to every technology
and is applicable for women of all ages, everywhere.

WEEK ONE
Committing to Yourself First

Your *Rules* Weekly Pep Talk

If you are reading this book, you are probably not the best at dating, have not found your lifelong partner, or are struggling to deal with people in healthier ways in your personal and professional relationships. We understand, and our intention is to guide and cheer you on each day for the next fifty-two weeks.

You may fantasize about romantic partners who don't initiate anything ("I'm just waiting for them to ask me out on a date."). You may pursue dates ("Want to grab coffee with me after work?") or act too available and eager when you do get asked out ("Love to . . . I'm free Tuesday, Thursday, and Friday after work and anytime this weekend . . . "). Who knew not to be so transparent? If this sounds like you, *The Rules Handbook* is for you!

Sometimes when you start dating, it seems easy because you're genuinely not interested in the person and they may not be your type. But then you do fall madly in love, and suddenly give your power away. You will lose your boundaries, become too casual, and see the person all the time. If you do this, the chase that began will stop. Your date suddenly becomes distant or wants space. Ouch! Stop, take a step back, and reset. Stop focusing on the person you're dating, and focus on nurturing and caring for yourself. For example, if you think, "I should send them a text about a vegetarian restaurant because we talked about plant-based food on our last date!" don't! Immediately switch your thoughts to, "What can I do to motivate myself so I am fulfilled and happier?" and DO THAT!

Many of our clients complain that between work, the gym, friends, and family, they have no time to do anything else. So we ask them, "Why use your valuable energy to send texts, remind others you exist, or show how often you're thinking about them?" You might think, *I just want to be friendly and connect.* No! If that person doesn't think about connecting with you, he might not be interested, and you might get hurt. Let him chase you!

COMMITTING TO YOURSELF FIRST
Daily *Rules*

Day 1: No More Rejection
MONDAY

Are you tired of getting hurt or rejected? Are you sick of
being single and spending another New Year's Eve or holiday
alone? Have you ever wondered why some women who
are not as attractive, smart, or nice as you are married and
you're not? Want to know their secret? They do *The Rules*!
They play hard to get; they don't talk to men first, ask them
out, act desperate, or seem overly interested. They have self-
esteem; have a happy, busy life; and date with boundaries.
Why not put following *The Rules* on a daily list along with all
your other goals and resolutions? Resolve to follow *The Rules*.

Day 2: Rules for Everyone
TUESDAY

While we originally wrote *The Rules* to help single women not
get hurt by men, we now realize you can practice *The Rules*
with everyone in your life. You might be happily dating or
married but get easily disappointed or hurt by family, friends,
coworkers, bosses, and even strangers. If so, remember to
follow *The Rules* to stay in your power, focus on yourself,
and wait for them to contact you first so you know they're
interested. We have found that our clients' other relationships
are much more successful when using "dating" rules. Why
initiate contact with people and risk being rejected? Why

pursue others when you can be sought after? Why share so much about yourself so quickly? Be more mysterious, slow down, and don't be an open book or in a hurry with everyone.

Day 3: Discipline
WEDNESDAY

Most women say they desire to become more disciplined. Their New Year's resolutions are typically to lose weight, exercise more, cut down on coffee, get their closets or papers or finances organized, go to bed earlier, and date. Yet when you suggest they follow a set of dos and don'ts for dating, they think that's crazy. Romance shouldn't be organized or disciplined. But if you're out of control in your relationships and give too much of yourself away by reaching out first or too often or texting too much, people will lose interest. Strategizing the most effective ways to date is no different from practicing any other healthy habits or setting goals.

Day 4: Lightbulb Moment
THURSDAY

Many readers around the world have told us they are grateful to have found *The Rules*. They tell us that before using *The Rules*, they were in the dark about why a relationship didn't work out. They said it was a lightbulb moment when they realized they were too available or needy with the people who wanted to date or be friends with them. They did not know there were effective relationship rules. They never considered who spoke to whom first, who ended the dates, or who paid. They never kept track of who called whom or how long the calls were. Everything was a blur! If you have been sleepwalking in your relationships for most of your life, it's time to turn on the lights, wake up, and learn *The Rules*!

Day 5: Fairy Godmother

FRIDAY

If your mother didn't tell you how to date or give you any guidance, then think of us as your fairy relationship godmothers. We will guide you on exactly what to do. We will not say, "You can do anything you want in life." We will say, "You can do anything you want in life, but it's not effective to pursue others without possibly getting hurt, so allow others to pursue you." We teach you how to become more confident and charming, how to dress in the way you feel most attractive, how to show up feeling more empowered, and how to gracefully end the date first so you leave others wanting to spend more time with you. Even if you didn't learn *The Rules* growing up or in high school or college, don't worry—you are lucky enough to be learning them in the following pages!

Day 6: Limit Social Media

SATURDAY

If you get easily hurt or jealous, we recommend you limit how much time you spend on social media. Seeing popular girls from high school who are still popular at thirty, forty, fifty, or sixty years old and posting fabulous photos of their husbands and children on vacation may feel like a knife in your heart if you are still single, childless, or married, poor, and definitely not yachting in Europe. It's like being in a bakery if you're on a diet or in a bar if you don't drink. Social media is not for the faint of heart. It can be a breeding ground for envy and self-pity (*Lower Self* thoughts), so venture at your own risk! When you limit your time on social media, you stop comparing yourself to others and spend that time living your own life. Search dating apps and attend singles events so you meet Mr. Right or new friends sooner. Read more inspirational books that offer healthier role models to help you to enhance your *Higher Self*.

Day 7: Don't Believe Everything You See

SUNDAY

Don't believe everything you see on Facebook and Instagram because it can be like living through high school all over again. Don't buy into it or believe all the seemingly flawless lifestyles of the rich and happy people you see online. Who knows if any of it's true? Remember, Facebook is often called "Fake Book"! Don't take all the posts and comments seriously either. We've seen couples posting picture-perfect photos and loving comments who are actually miserable or getting divorced. Be discerning about whom you follow on social media, as friending, following, or DMing someone on social media shows way too much interest in them. Keep the mystery and don't be easily available in between dates to show that you have a life. Constant contact kills the chase and makes others complacent. Let others follow you on Instagram first!

Apply *The Rules* to Achieve Your Higher Self

1   Instead of texting or calling him, call your mom or BFF!

2   Silence your phone and go to Pilates or for a walk!

3   Instead of confirming plans with him, make plans with yourself to get a mani-pedi!

WEEK TWO
Focus on the Inner You

Your *Rules* Weekly Pep Talk

This week, try to focus on becoming more confident and charming when practicing *The Rules*. Let go and forgive your parents, how you grew up, how you feel, or what you did last week, last night, or even five minutes ago, so you can grow and change and empower your *Higher Self*!

It doesn't matter if you had a difficult childhood with a cheating father or a critical mother or if you texted your ex-boyfriend ten times yesterday to get back together. Choose a different response and don't text him for the rest of the day. It's time to stop empowering the victim inside you and energize the heroine. Heal and release the damaged and desperate parts of you and start to enhance the confident and charming traits inside you. Don't fall into despair or think you're doomed based on your past track record. Get back up, and keep trying and transforming yourself.

Look for empowered role models around you, or throughout the world, of who you want to be more like. Write down all the character traits you admire and paint a picture of who you want to become. Emulate confident and self-focused people who are living their best lives, and the world will revolve around you not, others. Believe anything you envision is possible and that you are happy, healthy, and living your best life!

FOCUS ON THE INNER YOU
Daily *Rules*

Day 8: Higher versus Lower Self

MONDAY

Life can be a continuing battle of wits between your *Higher Self* and *Lower Self*, whether it's eating healthy food versus junk food, exercising or being a couch potato, or dating with self-control and confidence versus doing whatever you feel like. How do you motivate yourself and choose to empower your *Higher Self*? Do you want long-term satisfaction (a ring and a wedding date with a man who is crazy about you) or short-term gratification (a hookup or whirlwind courtship that fizzles out)? Do you want to have fun now or later? *The Rules* are not just about the here and now; they're about happily ever after.

Day 9: Perfectionism

TUESDAY

Are you a perfectionist? Are you waiting months or years to take just the right photos before posting your online profile? Perfectionism leads to procrastination and analysis paralysis. Anything worth doing is worth doing imperfectly right now. Perfectionism is really avoidance and a fear of rejection. Yes, there will be times when you will get rejected—that's life—but don't take anything personally. Be wise with what dating apps and social events you choose so you meet someone of quality and good character, but never avoid putting yourself out there. Are you posting a headshot and body shot and a brief profile such as "PrettyTrainer26...When I'm not working, I like to ski and watch the news..." on the way to the gym? Your profile should be light and breezy. Don't post twenty photos and tell your entire life story so there is no mystery about who you are! Better to try and fail once in a while with less, than not try at all or try way too hard.

Day 10: Inner Beauty

WEDNESDAY

An average-looking, confident person will attract a partner faster than an attractive person who is insecure. Who doesn't love a person with confidence? What person isn't looking for a partner with a sense of security and self-worth (*Higher Self*)? And who wants the opposite kind of person who is clingy and desperate (*Lower Self*)? Confidence is good character and inner beauty. So try to spend some time every day, even fifteen minutes, on nurturing your inside beauty, just as you do to your outer beauty. Exercise your brain, not just your body. Read anything that lifts your spirit and sense of self-worth, that reminds you that you are a Creature Unlike Any Other whom anyone would be lucky to date, marry, or hang out with!

Day 11: Inner Work

THURSDAY

In every relationship, it is most effective to focus on our own inner work. Too many people invest all their energy doing too much outer, physical work. They take the lead in a relationship by planning dates, driving, splitting the check, doing chores, and even buying gifts. They're exhausted, broke, and get little or nothing in return for so much external effort. A key rule is to invest your time and energy into yourself, which will empower you and make you more attractive. You will have little energy left to take the reins, call, text, plan dates, drive, or pay! Inner work leads to self-restraint, which yields the biggest payoff: courtship! Letting men take the lead in the dating and marriage dance will help you become more energized and desirable. It is far more attractive for a woman to receive than pursue!

Day 12: Project Confidence
FRIDAY

If you are not naturally confident—doubting your thoughts, your decisions, what you say, what you wear, whom you date—we have good news for you! You don't have to be born with confidence; you can gain it by practicing *The Rules Handbook* and having role models. Think of anyone you know who is naturally confident—the popular girl from high school, college, work or a celebrity—who is a natural *Rules Girl* that radiates beauty and self-esteem. Study how confident people walk into a room, talk, smile, laugh, and end conversations. Do not hesitate to emulate and learn from them. You don't have to act inauthentically or be fake, but enhance your own inner and outer beauty.

Day 13: Childhood Challenges
SATURDAY

You don't have to have had a healthy childhood to follow *The Rules*! Good or bad, your formative years don't have to define you. Don't think you are at a disadvantage with dating because of your dysfunctional or traumatic upbringing. You can heal those issues in therapy or possibly in private *Rules* consultations with us or one of our trained *Rules* coaches. Heal, forgive, and finally let go. But when it comes to dating, don't overshare—be self-controlled instead of reactive and show the most empowered parts of you. Don't tell a first date about how your prom date stood you up or the long list of dramas in your life. This unhealthy sharing is motivated by you wanting to feel understood and seen, but it is actually inappropriate in the first few months of dating. Transparency is overrated. Eventually, the person will know everything about you.

Day 14: Believing
SUNDAY

You can never go wrong by being hopeful. Try believing in the possibility of your future soulmate. Women who are bitter about their exes or about being alone attract more bad luck. Women who believe in good luck attract more of that. But you can't just believe and do nothing. Tell yourself "I believe" while you are walking out the door with your ski poles or tennis racquet, or to a bar or speed-dating event!

Apply *The Rules* to Achieve Your Higher Self

1 Instead of taking more photos for your dating profile, post the most flattering pics you already have! The sooner, the better.

2 Don't compare yourself to Instagram models half your age or with a ton of filters; just put on a touch of makeup and run to the gym!

3 Put happy love songs on your playlist to inspire you.

WEEK THREE

Appreciating the Outer You

Your *Rules* Weekly Pep Talk

This week, we encourage you to focus on appreciating and taking care of the outer you! Pick three physical qualities about yourself that you love. Green eyes? Smile? Wavy hair? Consider what beauty means to you and what attributes you admire. Make another list of three things you can do to enhance your own beauty, such as sit-ups, facials, and a makeover.

We acknowledge this might be hard for most people reading this book, because all of us have our own insecurities about our looks or a long list of how we want to change our bodies and images. But we encourage you to take little actions towards improving how you look, so you build more confidence and feel more empowered in your own person.

Evaluate the people surrounding you who constantly put themselves down or can't take a compliment. Do you find these people attractive? Maybe you're the President of the *I Hate Myself Club*. Is this who you want to be? Or maybe you are self-deprecating and a *Saturday Night Live* Debbie Downer-type. Might one of these people be you? Now, we're not saying to be egomaniacal, overly self-confident, or think you're God's gift to men either. Just be the right-sized version of you. This week, focus on becoming your own cheerleader or coach. Think, recite, or write positive affirmations like, "I'm pretty enough. I'm smart enough. I'm good enough! I was born to create my joy in life, and I deserve to be loved, cherished, and respected. I have value and purpose just as I am, and any man would be lucky to meet, spend time with, date, and get to know me!"

APPRECIATING THE OUTER YOU
Daily *Rules*

Day 15: Invisible Tiara
MONDAY

Women are often their harshest critics. They berate themselves for having large thighs or other unattractive body
parts or for breaking *The Rules* when they know better. They
say things like, "My face is fat!" or "I'm too tall or short,"
or "I'm so stupid. I can't believe I had so much to drink
and slept with him." If you're your biggest critic, you still
have some outer nurturing to do and encouragement to give
yourself, and maybe it's time to fire the President of the *I Hate
(Your Name) Club.* Tell yourself several times each day, "I am
a Creature Unlike Any Other!" Repeat to yourself, "I am
beautifully and wonderfully made!" Create an invisible tiara
and visualize it on your head at all times so you can feel and
expect others to love you, even during moments when you
don't particularly like or love yourself.

Day 16: Choose Clothing That Empowers You
TUESDAY

Thanks to COVID, activewear, hoodies, leggings, yoga
pants, pajama bottoms, and other casual clothes have
become the norm. Some women feel that it's fine to wear
loungewear and UGG boots on dates. Well, we're sorry, but
we disagree. Comfortable clothes and footwear are fine for
walking your dog, grocery shopping, or doing chores, but

when you're going on a date or to a social event, you want to feel more empowered and look like the best version of yourself. We recommend a classic, simple, but sexy style: a scoop or V-neck top can be enchanting; skinny jeans or miniskirts will make you feel and look sexier; and high heels and hoop earrings will make you feel more youthful. When you follow *The Rules* recommended dress code, you'll look and feel more attractive to yourself as well as to others!

Day 17. What You Wear Can Transform You
WEDNESDAY

In a makeover coaching consultation with a client, we suggested she buy over-the-knee boots, but she thought they were a little pricey. She debated about whether to buy them until she noticed that there was only one size nine left. In that instant, she was inspired because she envisioned how she would look and feel in the boots and immediately bought them. Suddenly, money was no object, only how attractive she felt wearing her new boots! Most everyone wants to improve their appearance but needs motivation—snooze and you lose in this case. Everyone wants what they can't have or almost can't have. The way this client felt about the last pair of size nine boots is how other people should feel about you. If they don't take action fast, someone else will snap you up! So make positive choices that empower you to feel more confident and beautiful. Take pride in your appearance!

Day 18: Entitled versus Down-to-Earth
THURSDAY

Don't assume that a happy childhood makes you automatically charming. Some women from lovely homes with adoring parents and no financial issues have other problems. They may have been given everything material they ever wanted and act entitled. So much of their self-worth comes from material things. They are annoyed if the guy doesn't take them to a four-star restaurant, or they turn up their noses if he doesn't wear designer loafers or order expensive champagne. They are not humble or nice. It's impossible to please them. Some only want to date men with sports cars. People who follow *The Rules* have high self-esteem but are also down-to-earth and realistic. They care more about character than a credit card. What about you?

Day 19: Clarity
FRIDAY

Women who don't know how they gained twenty pounds do not differ from women who don't know why their relationship took a turn for the worst. They're in a fog. They lack clarity. We suggest keeping a food or dating clarity log. Write down how many calories you consumed or who spoke to whom first, who traveled to whom, who suggested what, who paid, and so on. Knowledge is power. When you know where you are not sticking to *The Rules*, you can get back on track again.

Day 20: Dress Confidently

SATURDAY

Some of the smartest women who are accountants, doctors, lawyers, and MBAs don't know how to dress for dating! They dress the same on dates as when hanging out with friends or walking or hiking: leggings, sports bras, warm puffy jackets, turtlenecks, billowy scarves, flat shoes or clogs or combat boots, fanny packs and tote bags, with boring unisex smart watches. They certainly don't dress for potential partners who like a little sizzle with their steak! Their clothes scream comfortable, not attractive or sexy. They mistakenly believe that their personality and intellect are the only part of the dating package. We remind them that their looks ignite the fire before their date desires to discover their inner selves. We recommend our clients wear more flattering clothing and accessories for their dating app photos and meetups. And if possible, we also encourage people who are dating to wear makeup to highlight their own beauty. The difference is dramatic, and they get more dates!

Day 21: Try Your Best Not to Force Anything

SUNDAY

Don't invite yourself to any social situations or get angry if people leave you out. If you are part of a texting group chat, ask everyone if they're free to meet, no one answers, and then you see a Facebook post of them out with the tagline, "Gang's all here!" don't furiously text, *Hey what's going on? Why did you go out without me?* It will make you seem insecure and pushy. Don't force yourself on a group. Either accept you're not always going to be invited or find another group. Tell yourself rejection is life's protection. There's a reason you were not supposed to be there—believe that there are better and kinder friends out there for you!

Apply *The Rules* to Achieve Your Higher Self

1 Every time you have a critical thought about yourself ("huge thighs"), immediately replace it with a positive thought ("big green eyes").

2 Wear form-fitting clothes on dates, not loose loungewear.

3 The same way you record your food in a journal or app, record your dating habits (who spoke or messaged whom first; the length of calls, text chats, and dates; and who ended what first).

How You Present Yourself Matters

Your *Rules* Weekly Pep Talk

This week, we want you to consider how you present yourself in the mirror and then to others. First, you need to feel confident when you walk out the door. Second, consider that when you meet others, either planned or unexpectedly, you may never get a second chance to make a good first impression.

Don't think, "No one is going to see me, so who cares?" Please care! Always consider, I could run into my future partner at the gym, a new boyfriend at the post office, or a new best friend at a local coffee shop. What impression do you want to make on the world?

The more empowered you feel about who you are, what you are wearing, and what you look like, the more confident you'll feel and act. So before you present yourself to others or post anything on social media, please make sure that you look your best confident self. You may feel your most beautiful, natural self in casual clothes, with blown-out hair or a hint of makeup, or wearing a trendy outfit or your favorite pair of shoes. You get to choose—so make it fun and you are sure to look radiant!

HOW YOU PRESENT YOURSELF MATTERS
Daily *Rules*

Day 22: Beauty Isn't Enough
MONDAY

You would think that gorgeous actresses and models wouldn't need *The Rules*, that people are falling all over them and their calendar is always full. Yes, and no. Because they are beautiful, they have no problem meeting others, but keeping them is another story. Whether you are a beauty queen or an average-looking person, you still need a dating strategy to make you seem slightly unattainable and more desirable. It won't matter what you look like in the long run. Whoever follows *The Rules* has a better chance of finding and keeping the person they love, much more than a celebrity or supermodel who doesn't. You can't coast solely on your looks!

Day 23: Thank the Academy
TUESDAY

When you are feeling particularly unattractive, have bags under your eyes, or your skin is blotchy and you want to stay in bed, think again. Instead, why don't you put on makeup and a full-length gown, stand in front of a mirror with a fake microphone (a cell phone or a big perfume bottle will do), and "Thank the Academy...!" Pretend you're a movie star. Stop looking at old photos regretfully while wearing sweatpants. Replace the bad and self-defeating feelings with positive thoughts. As cosmetics icon Helena Rubinstein quipped, "There are no ugly women, only lazy ones."

Day 24: Keep It Light
WEDNESDAY

Use social media sparingly to post only attractive photos and post with the fewest words possible. Don't use it as a podium for pet peeves, complaining, or politics. It's unbecoming, and you'll look like you have too much time on your hands. Post meaningful photos of your life that make you shine, but don't post every day or comment incessantly. Don't get involved in online group fights! It will suck the life out of you. Take nothing anyone else says or does personally. Don't be overly sensitive or mad at the world or Facebook community. If you meet someone and they say, "Friend me!", wait twenty-four hours. And if they ignore your request, pretend you never met them and move on!

Day 25: Don't Be the Post Police
THURSDAY

Don't hesitate to post pretty photos online because you're afraid other people might think you're being conceited. If you're lucky enough to have pretty photos, go for it. Don't be a people-pleaser. Similarly, don't tell other people what to post and not post on social media. Maybe you find your friend's endless political rants or perfect sunset posts annoying and you want to tell her to "Get a life!" or "Get a job!" Don't! Don't lose a friend over social media. Some people just morph into another person on Facebook, much like an actress on a stage, but they are still good friends in real life!

Day 26: Mystery

FRIDAY

Most people love to talk, but potential partners love mystery! So when a date calls, don't tell him everything in detail that happened to you this week, this month, or this year. Most women have an intense need to communicate. Most men don't, so the more you share in small doses, the better. Thinking that having deep conversations will draw you closer together is a common misconception. Too much talking can have the opposite effect. He will feel bored. Don't worry, you will share more of yourself over time. This is not being fake. It's just respectful and honoring your *Higher Self*. You are interviewing to date—it's similar to a job interview, so don't overshare (*Lower Self*). Ditto for dating!

Day 27: Drinking and Dating Don't Mix

SATURDAY

Being a *Rules Girl* is like being sober at a party where everyone else is drunk. While other girls are having fun flirting with guys and hooking up, it's easy to feel you're missing out. We get it! We didn't write *The Rules* to restrict or ruin your life but to transform you from unconscious dating to self-awareness and mindfulness, from helter-skelter to results-oriented *Higher Self* behavior. We wrote *The Rules* to help you find a man who will fall madly in love with you, be committed, and put a ring on it. The hardest challenge will be overcoming your *Lower Self*, which wants short-term fun at any cost. Real fun is dating the right person who becomes a committed boyfriend, then a husband, and not a one-night stand.

Day 28: Perseverance over Prettiness

SUNDAY

The race doesn't always go to the swiftest! Similarly, the prettiest girl doesn't always get the guy. Sometimes the prettiest girl doesn't do *The Rules* because she feels looks are all it takes to attract a potential partner or that dating apps and singles events are beneath her *Lower Self*. But a less pretty girl who perseveres, who stays on dating apps and goes to singles events and on blind dates, who asks everyone to introduce her to guys, and who plods along and is her humble, *Higher Self* is successful because she didn't give up! Are you pretty but lacking in perseverance?

Apply *The Rules* to Achieve Your Higher Self

1 Try not to drink alcohol on dates, but if you're in the mood, limit yourself to one drink. Women who drink too much end up oversharing or becoming intimate too soon.

2 Be careful how you present yourself in real life and on social media. Look pretty, post your best photos, and don't talk or write too much so you remain elusive.

3 Don't think that physical attraction is enough to keep a guy interested. It's enough to meet a guy, but keeping him requires playing a little hard to get!

WEEK FIVE
Become More Self-Confident

Your *Rules* Weekly Pep Talk

This week, focus on being confident but realistic, meaning that you can keep your head in the clouds but have your feet firmly planted on the ground. So while you believe that you're a Creature Unlike Any Other and any man would be lucky to date and spend time with you, you realize that he won't just show up and knock on your front door. You need to put your most confident self out into the world where there is a possibility of meeting someone.

Once you own your worth and go out into the world of dating, don't be naïve. When you leave the house to socialize and meet people you connect with to date, be confident but not delusional. Don't make up and fantasize that your date likes you more than they are saying or expressing, or you will get hurt. Stop entertaining the idea that your dentist, coworker, or neighbor has a secret crush on you and that one day he will find the courage to ask you out on a date, even though he has never asked you out in the five years he's known you.

Be real, be honest, and read the dating signs clearly so you don't get your hopes up and expect too much from a person whose actions or words don't show they truly care about you.

BECOME MORE SELF-CONFIDENT
Daily *Rules*

Day 29: Dating is a Decision
MONDAY

Confidence is not just a feeling or a fleeting thought—it is the right attitude followed by action, a decision. Many women claim that they're 100% committed to finding their soulmates, but when we ask if they signed up on any online dating sites, they say, "Um, no, that's not for me. I'm very visible at my job and would be mortified if my coworkers saw me online. They would think I was desperate." So we nicely explain, "If your coworkers saw you online, then they are online too, and obviously if it's okay for them, then it's okay for you! More importantly, why do you care what other people think of you?"

Day 30: Not Interested
TUESDAY

Some people have too much confidence in the wrong way. They are convinced that their neighbor, coworker, financial planner, dentist, or lawyer is interested in them. When we ask, "Has he ever asked you out?" they reply, "No," and then we find out this imaginary dance has been going on for months or years. We tell them that, unfortunately, he is not interested. It's a fantasy relationship if he doesn't ask you out. He is not shy. He's not getting over his ex. He is not too busy with work, or not this or that—he's just not interested.

Following you on Instagram or watching your stories or TikToks or talking to you as a patient or coworker is not enough. Following up on business is not enough. He has to ask you out and show clear signs of interest.

Day 31: Everything but . . .

WEDNESDAY

Women often tell us they have everything they want in life—a great career, apartment, friends, and hobbies—but they can't meet a date. When we ask what they are doing to meet men, they claim they have no time because they are doctors, lawyers, MBAs, and businesswomen. We ask, "Well, what do you do when you're not working?" They say, "Go to the gym, go to the movies with girlfriends, or see family." We reply, "If you really want to get married, make meeting men your top priority. In your spare time, you should be responding to messages on your dating apps and going to parties, cool bars, clubs, and singles events such as hiking or speed dating! Dating has to be first, or it's last! You can see your friends and family at your wedding!"

Day 32: Reaching Out Rationalizations

THURSDAY

Even the most business-savvy woman will try to convince herself that the reason a date didn't reach out after a first or second date is that, (a) she didn't offer to help pay for drinks, appetizers, or dinner, (b) she ended the date after two hours, (c) she did *The Rules* too strictly by not talking enough or acting more enthusiastic, (d) she didn't let them up to her apartment or sleep together, or (e) she didn't text "Thank you" the next day. She will seek out five girlfriends to agree with her rationale. An otherwise intelligent woman's ability to lie to herself (*Lower Self*) so she can reach out to a date, despite knowing *The Rules* backwards and forwards, is mind-boggling. She can be the toughest negotiator in advertising, sales, or real estate, but she completely falls apart when she doesn't hear from a date the next day. We have to talk her off the ledge to not text him at all and remind her that her *Higher Self* will regret it. At the very least, we advise her to put off the urge to text him for twenty-four hours. You can do anything for one day.

Day 33: A Lost Art

FRIDAY

Being charming is a lost art! Women today are bombarded with messages to be badasses and seductresses. They are encouraged to go on dating apps and make the first move. They are told to be obvious and aggressive. One relationship expert suggested that just the way Victorian women used to drop their handkerchiefs in front of men to get their attention, women today should show interest by making eye contact, standing in close proximity, and being more approachable by getting off their phones. The truth is, men don't need extra encouragement if they are interested in asking you out. Do nothing but show up!

Day 34: Teflon
SATURDAY

Being charming is being Teflon. It's being pleasant, polite, self-controlled, and easy to be with (*Higher Self*). It's not being sarcastic, jealous, or easily offended (*Lower Self*). It's impossible to be angry and charming at the same time. You can't be mean and expect a guy to stick around. Tell yourself that nothing bothers you or pretend that nothing bothers you. If you think your date is taking forever to order his meal, don't say, "I'm starving. What's taking you so long?" Or, if you think he's looking at the waitress, please don't comment, "Maybe you want to go out with her instead?" Don't say everything that pops into your head, especially if it's hostile or unattractive!

Day 35: Not Desperate
SUNDAY

Some women say they are definitely "intentional" about dating, that their goal this year is to meet and marry Mr. Right. But it's all talk and no action. They claim they tried dating apps and found them disappointing, so they deleted them or canceled their subscriptions. They claim they don't enjoy going out at night to bars and clubs or speed-dating events, nor do they care for hiking or skiing or tennis; and they don't belong to a church or temple, and they really prefer reading or watching TV after work. So basically, they are doing nothing to meet men, and that's why they're still single. We advise them that's not intentional—that's lazy.

You have to get out of your comfort zone or you'll be alone.
You can read and watch TV when you're married!

Apply *The Rules* to Achieve Your Higher Self

1   No matter how terrible your last five online dates were or how hopeless you feel, don't delete your dating apps. You have to be in the dating game to win it!

2   Don't be perfectionistic about your online pics. Most guys are looking for the girl next door, not a Barbie doll.

3   On dates, don't forget to be feminine. No eye rolling or being annoyed at the server.

WEEK SIX

Preparing Yourself Mentally
for *The Rules*

Your *Rules* Weekly Pep Talk

This week, we would like you to mentally prepare for how difficult following *The Rules* will be. It may be hard to adjust from the way you were dating—free and following no rules—to how we recommend you date: carefully with clear-cut instructions. It is going to take every ounce of willpower and discipline for you to muster to follow what some people think are controversial rules.

There will be times in your life when you go out just to have fun and aren't looking for any serious relationship. That is fine, but if you are looking for a serious relationship and later on marriage, then doing *The Rules* will only work if you can stay in your power, know your value, and don't allow your world to revolve around the person you are dating, especially if you are crazy about him and want to marry him.

Many women go on dates and then complain that the guy they like doesn't like them (or vice versa) or there was no chemistry. All the more reason, when you do meet a potential Mr. Right, to follow *The Rules*. Be your best self, be charming and mysterious, and be the one to end dates, phone calls, and texts first to leave them wanting more. Men love to hunt, but if you leave a dead deer on their doorstep, they'll be bored.

PREPARING YOURSELF MENTALLY FOR *THE RULES*
Daily *Rules*

Day 36: Nurture Yourself
MONDAY

Many women are nurturers, which is a compassionate quality, but not for dating. Save any acts of service like writing
their college paper or decorating their apartment for when
you are engaged or married. These selfless gestures may
come across as desperate and overstepping. Your dates will
sense that you are overbearing and "hard selling" them on
falling in love with you. The truth is, you need to do very
little but show up on dates to make another person fall in
love with you. If you feel like nurturing them, nurture yourself. Take a bubble bath, get a manicure, or clean your own
apartment!

Day 37: Don't Act Insecure
TUESDAY

Are you insecure (*Lower Self*)? It will not serve you to show
your boyfriend or husband this part of you very often. Share
it with us, your therapist, or best friends. Too many women
in a weak moment will ask their significant other, "Are you
happy with me?" or "Why are you even with me?" No matter how badly you feel about yourself, such words should
never leave your lips. Even on your worst day, don't let your
partner see your *Lower Self*. Not only is it unflattering because
you're a Creature Unlike Any Other and any man would be

lucky to be with you, but it's self-centered and needy. If you need attention or validation, get affirmations from your family and friends or life coach. Most men have simple needs, and they want you to be happy and appreciate your time together.

Day 38: Turnoffs
WEDNESDAY

There are certain qualities that are the opposite of confidence that turn other people off, such as insecurity, jealousy, people-pleasing, anger, control, pushiness, and not taking a hint or reading the room. It's normal to feel any or all of the above in a relationship, but just make sure you don't act out on it. For example, if you're afraid because a guy ghosted you, don't text him, "Is everything okay? I haven't heard from you all week!" Don't keep the relationship going by saying, "You treated last time. Why don't I take you out next time?" Hello! He doesn't like you, hence why he didn't ask you out again. Paying won't change how he feels. Next!

Day 39: Law of Attraction
THURSDAY

If you are looking for Prince Charming as a soulmate, you need to be charming yourself! It's the law of attraction. Many women make a checklist of what they want in a partner: charismatic, successful, financially stable, generous, funny, athletic, and empathetic. But they forget to check their own boxes first. Are you charming? Are you successful? Are you generous? Are you in good shape? Are you a good listener? If you want all these qualities in a partner, develop these qualities in yourself. The sooner you empower your *Higher Self*, the sooner you will meet your soulmate!

Day 40: Love Addiction
FRIDAY

Are you addicted to love? Do you feel a constant craving to contact a man, to talk with him, to text him, and to spend endless time with him? Some women are in love with love, in the same way some people are addicted to drinking or shopping. If so, you don't have to spend ten years in therapy to stop this behavior. *The Rules* can be your cure. Use your *Higher Self* to not text him incessantly or see him all the time or blurt out all your feelings. *The Rules* will give you permission to set limits and have a well-rounded life. If you find following *The Rules* hard on your own, we offer private *Rules* coaching that may help you heal your love addiction.

Day 41: Boring over Bad
SATURDAY

Some women complain that doing *The Rules* is boring! Who cares if it's boring if it works? We understand it's hard *not* to take action by talking to your cute male coworkers first, inviting your new neighbor over for coffee, asking a handsome stranger at the bar if he's been there before, friending men on Facebook, or following guys on Instagram. And it's even harder when your non-*Rules* friends seem to be having the time of their lives! They're meeting guys left and right, having marathon-long dates, late text chats that go into the middle of the night, hookups, and going on weeklong trips. They're Venmo-ing guys half of the airplane fare and hotel bills and inviting new guys to be their plus-one to their office Christmas party or sister's wedding! Busy, busy, but all this non-*Rules* behavior will eventually boomerang! Don't be jealous because it's not a competition, and don't worry because whatever they're doing won't last. Remember, it's not about quantity, but quality. You only want one good guy who wants you, not five guys who are lukewarm or not interested. Better to be busy with work, hobbies, dating apps, and social events to meet new men than to make anything happen.

Day 42: Overcoming Fear

SUNDAY

Do you have social anxiety? Are you afraid of showing up and meeting men because you don't know what to say or because you've had hurtful experiences in the past or not-the-best relationship with your father? Are you afraid of rejection or disappointment? While all the above may be valid, your fear of being single has to be greater than your fear of anything else. Your fear of being alone forever has to trump your fear and motivate you to make small talk at a party with a man who approaches you or to go out on a date. Sometimes the only way to overcome a fear is to be more afraid of not doing the very thing you fear.

Apply *The Rules* to Achieve Your Higher Self

1   Make a list of everything you want in a partner, and then be that person!

2   Share your insecurities with a dating coach or your BFF, not him!

3   Be more afraid of being alone than being on dating apps or social events.

WEEK SEVEN
Committing to *The Rules*

Your *Rules* Weekly Pep Talk

This week, we want you to take a deep breath, review *The Rules*, and then commit to following as many of *The Rules* as you can to the best of your ability. For most people, it will be difficult when you first begin, but like exercise or changing any unhealthy habit, it takes trial-and-error and starts-and-stops with lots of practice in between!

We understand that most people have so many decisions to make every day, like how to balance work and dating, how to fit in the gym, how much money to save versus spend, and so on. The last thing they need to worry about is a new set of rules to follow. It may be a challenge to decide whether you should text a guy to confirm a date, offer to split the check, or end the date early. We take away all that guesswork. Once you understand the beauty of *The Rules* and how effective your new way of responding during and in between dates will be, you will dive all in because *The Rules* are time-tested and a foolproof formula.

Why not have one area of your life that is figured out for you so you don't have to keep second-guessing how to reply to phone calls, texts, or emails? Or if you should make the first move and invite someone out on a date? When in doubt about what to do, reread and review *The Rules*!

COMMITTING TO *THE RULES*
Daily *Rules*

Day 43: No More Guesswork
MONDAY

Are you tired of well-meaning dating advice from friends
and family members that doesn't work? Have you had it
with do-whatever-you-darn-well-please suggestions from
your peers and twentysomething-year-old social media
influencers? Are you fed up with so-called dating coaches
who tell you to call men, ask them out, and pay for dates
because . . . hey, why not? Are you sick of losing years to
commitment-phobes and time-wasters and being burnt by
Buyer Beware partners? Did you graduate from high school
and college but never learn about courtship? Do you wonder
when it's best to go to his place, let your date come to your
home, or become intimate? Do these basic questions roll
around in your mind, keeping you up at night? Commit
yourself to studying *The Rules Handbook*!

Day 44: Disingenuous or Genius?
TUESDAY

Perhaps doing *The Rules* seems kind of fake. Why not text
someone if you feel like texting? Why not pay if you make
more money or feel generous? Why not travel to his area if
he's in an exciting city and you live in the boondocks? Why
not say you're in love first if you feel he is The One? Why not
be intimate on the first date if you're in the mood? Why hold

back? Why not lay all your cards on the table and tell him about your dysfunctional childhood or divorce if he asks? Because doing all of the above will stop the chase, which will make you feel insecure. We all love intrigue and mystery, so don't be an open book. Remember, you're the more sensitive one, the one who gets more easily hurt or devastated when a relationship doesn't work out. After all, you're the one reading *The Rules Handbook!* They certainly are not!

Day 45: Embrace Your Higher Self

WEDNESDAY

Saying "No" when you really want to say "Yes!" might seem difficult, especially when you're not busy or self-confident. We hear from many clients, "I'm not an actress, so how can I lie about turning down a last-minute date?" or "What if he knows I'm not doing anything?" It doesn't matter if he does, and we doubt he ever will. Washing your hair is doing something. Reading a book or going to the gym is doing something. Not seeing him is doing something. You don't have to go to Europe to be busy. You just have to be disciplined and use your *Higher Self* to not be easily available. Follow the once-a-week (Wednesday for Saturday night) dating maximum plan for the first month, end of story. Backsliding into seeing him all the time (*Lower Self*) will ruin the dating dance and your self-esteem. Remember, you're teaching a man how to treat you. If you accept his last-minute dates, he will treat you last minute and not value you!

Day 46: Transparency is Overrated
THURSDAY

The latest buzzwords in the self-help genre are authenticity and transparency. While we believe in being honest, we don't believe in oversharing or saying everything we think. What if your authentic self wants to text him all day or send balloons to his office for his promotion? What if the transparent part of you wants to get angry when you don't hear from him for a few days? Such authenticity, transparency, and intensity can scare anyone away. We believe in being self-controlled, in choosing to empower your *Higher Self* over your *Lower Self*.

Day 47: Don't Complain or Interrupt
FRIDAY

Complaining or interrupting on a date is the equivalent of chalk screeching on a blackboard. Who wants to hear or experience a toxic conversation? To be a charming person is to ignore annoyances and stay in your power no matter what happens. If the food is bland or the server takes forever to refill your water, ask nicely again. Don't throw a fit if your date forgets where he parked his car and you're wearing heels. If the flowers he bought you look like they came from a gas station, graciously say, "Thanks, they're beautiful." If you interrupt your date, it means you're not concentrating on or caring about what the other person is saying—you just want to hear yourself speak or think what you have to say is more important. Don't be one of those people who is thinking about what she wants to say instead of listening to what the other person is saying. If you talk less on a date, you can learn more about him, and it will impress him that you're a good listener.

Day 48: Self-Sabotage

SATURDAY

Women sabotage their relationships when they show their anger and selfishness (*Lower Self*). For example, a client got upset that her divorced boyfriend ended a date early because he found out at the last minute that he could see his children and because he didn't invite her to be his plus-one on a business trip. We had to coach her on understanding the root of and overcoming her insecurities and immature behavior. A man wants a woman who is happy and busy—not needy or demanding, not in competition with his kids, and not someone who invites herself on trips or interrogates him about his photos on Facebook or female friendships. Leave your *Lower Self* at home when you go on dates and empower your *Higher Self.*

Day 49: Choosing to Be Your Higher Self

SUNDAY

Choosing to share your *Higher Self* versus your *Lower Self* does not just apply to romantic relationships, but to every aspect of your life. Every thought and action you choose is often a struggle between long-term satisfaction and short-term gratification. Going to the gym versus staying in bed, working versus surfing the internet, donating to charity versus hoarding, making dinner for your partner's family or friends versus saying, "Didn't we just see them?" The harder choice is usually the right decision. If you always take the easier path, your relationship will be mediocre instead of exceptional.

Apply *The Rules* to Achieve Your Higher Self

1   Resolve to do one hard *Higher Self* action today, such as not texting him and going to the gym. Don't ask if *The Rules* are retro or fake; ask yourself if they're working.

2   Put a rubber band on your wrist, and every time you want to indulge in *Lower Self* behavior, such as complaining or interrupting, pull the rubber band! Ouch!

3   When you want to complain to your date, think of something positive to say.

WEEK EIGHT
Practicing *The Rules*

Your *Rules* Weekly Pep Talk

Are you ready to implement *The Rules* into your life? This week, focus on dating by *The Rules* as your top priority, not an afterthought. Don't squeeze in practicing *The Rules* after playing pickleball, traveling, shopping, surfing your Instagram account, or fill in the blank with the many other excuses you can make to avoid practicing.

It's been two months since you started reading and studying these Weekly Pep Talks and Daily Lessons. We have confidence that you are ready to implement all you have learned on your dates. It's time to put yourself out there, and it's time to be all in!

Women who wake up every three months or every year and decide to go on one dating app or date have little or nothing to show for it and are not following *The Rules*. *The Rules* are about consistency and persistence, not dabbling. Now that you know better, you can do better at putting yourself out into the dating world! Make dating a regular habit, like going to the gym.

To begin, go out once a week and try to increase to three times a week. Try attending singles events and going to local clubs, restaurants, or friendly bars. Ask family and friends if they know anybody who might be a good match for you and have them set you up on a date. Don't give up and don't stop going out until you meet your "person" and future marriage partner.

PRACTICING *THE RULES*
Daily *Rules*

Day 50: Practice *The Rules*
MONDAY

If you want to get good at *The Rules*, you're going to have to live and breathe them. When you talk to women and the topic of dating comes up, ask them how they met their boyfriends or husbands. When you watch TV shows and movies or read about celebrity relationships, look for *The Rules* and non-*Rules* behavior. Who spoke to whom first? Who pursued whom? How did it work out? In photos, is the man leaning into the woman or is she all over him? But, don't believe most romantic comedies like *Something's Gotta Give*, in which a woman breaks every rule and still gets the guy. That only happens in Hollywood movies, never in real life!

Day 51: Work Now, Fun Later
TUESDAY

The Rules may seem like a lot of work in the beginning. You are counting the minutes or hours to text back, ending dates first, seeing him only once a week in the first month, not getting intimate too soon, not splitting the bill or buying him gifts or cooking him dinner or showing up at his place unannounced. You are doing less than you ever have in a relationship and are wondering how exactly this self-deprivation plan is going to work. Don't worry, it will exceed your wildest dreams when you meet and marry your life partner! The real world is all about excess and spur-of-the-moment pleasure. *The Rules'* world is about less fun now, but long-lasting love later!

Day 52: Like Job Hunting

WEDNESDAY

Women tell us they want to meet their soulmates, but when we ask them what actions they are taking, they tell us they don't have time, it will happen when it happens, or they don't believe in dedicated singles events. They want to meet men naturally at the gym, at work, or at the dog park. If only it were that easy! We explain that after college, meeting guys naturally is incredibly rare. You have to go to upscale bars, speed dating, and other singles events. You would never expect to find a job "naturally." You need to network, send out resumes, and show up for interviews. As unromantic as it sounds, dating is like job hunting.

Day 53: Courtship Isn't Dead

THURSDAY

If you want to feel more confident about dating or getting married, try not to read or think about anything negative on the subject. Many newspaper articles over the last two decades have declared that courtship is dead, citing the fact that more men want to hang out and not commit. A Rules Girl reading this wouldn't put away her short spandex skirt, hoop earrings, and heels so fast! Nor should she! Upon closer examination, all the women quoted in these articles were *Rules*-breakers who traveled to men or indulged in text chats or sexting, and so, of course, they didn't experience courtship. Courtship is alive and well for Rules Girls!

Day 54: Parental Advice

FRIDAY

When we do consultations, we typically ask clients if their parents taught them anything about dating. Many claim that there was little guidance on the subject and more emphasis on going to college and their careers. But in some cases, parents mentioned "playing hard to get" or gave them our first book, *The Rules*. Almost always our clients thought their parents were being ridiculous or old-fashioned and didn't take their advice. They argued, "It's different now. You don't know what you're talking about." Interestingly, the same women who scoffed are now die-hard *Rules* followers, calling us for consultations. Regardless of whether you were told about *The Rules* growing up or just found out about them today, you know it now. When you know how to react better, you change your behavior and do better!

Day 55: Married Creature Unlike Any Other

SATURDAY

When you were dating, we told you to be a Creature Unlike Any Other, confident and self-controlled, enchanting and easy to be with. Being a CUAO doesn't stop when you're in a committed relationship, engaged, or married. A married CUAO is just as lovely to be around! She doesn't compare herself to other people (*Lower Self*). She won't compare her husband to other husbands, like some catty wives do. She doesn't say, "Mark just became a partner and is driving a Mercedes, and his wife had a face-lift . . . One of the reasons I married you is because you were ambitious and would be a good provider. Was that just for show?" On the contrary, she's his biggest cheerleader. "You're going to kill it in that interview." A married CUAO is a happy camper!

Day 56: As Long as Possible

SUNDAY

Many women wonder how long they have to follow *The Rules*. The answer is as long as possible, but definitely in the first crucial three months because that's when a potential partner is deciding if they love you and want to marry you. Have you ever noticed that most guys are rarely busy at the beginning of a relationship? They're busy later on when you become demanding, entitled, or clingy. That's why we suggest doing *The Rules* for the entire relationship while gradually letting him know more about you by the time he proposes. Women who stop doing *The Rules* too soon complain that their boyfriends are not committing. That's because they stopped doing *The Rules*.

Apply *The Rules* to Achieve Your Higher Self

1   When you go to a party or watch a movie, pretend you're a sociologist and look for *The Rules* and non-*Rules* behavior. Notice which women are flitting around the room versus being clingy. Copy the flitters, the Rules Girls!

2   Don't read anything negative about courtship. It's alive and well for a Rules Girl!

3   If you miss a guy and want to call him to hear his voice, call your mother!

COURSE 2

Navigating New Relationships

10 WEEKS

Whether you're in a new relationship or trying to get back with an ex, it's best to keep your faith in love and courtship (*Higher Self*) and not be negative or cynical (*Lower Self*). Don't think "Dating is different now; everything is last-minute and mutual," or "All the good men are taken." Traditional courtship still exists, and there are plenty of good men out there! So change your thinking and behavior if you don't want to get the same old poor results! As Albert Einstein said, "Insanity is doing the same thing over and over and expecting different results."

Most clients tell us they don't have a problem playing hard to get in the very beginning by letting men make the first move in person or online, but after a few dates, *The Rules* go out the window. They start texting men interesting article links or inviting them over for popcorn and Netflix or as their plus-one to their cousin's wedding. Before they know it, the guy is asking for space or ghosts them. If you don't want this to happen to you, don't initiate anything. Let the guy do all texting, asking out, suggesting, and sending links and photos for the entire courtship. You can respond, but you can't initiate without risking rejection.

It's up to you to change and use *The Rules* as your key tools to become the empowered woman a man wants to spend the rest of his life with! You can also use these invaluable tools when you want to get an ex back. First, we have to find out who spoke to whom first. If you initially pursued him online or in person, forget him. He never liked you that much or never thought of you as a potential life partner, so it's done. But if he made the first move and broke up with you because you got clingy, then you can text him once for closure. Write something like, "Just wanted to say sorry I was difficult (or fill in the blank), happy holidays and hope is well!" If he doesn't write back, next! If he writes back but doesn't suggest meeting to talk about it, next! Never write to him again. But if he writes back, "Thanks, do you want to get together for drinks?" Bingo! You can meet up and be your best self, the girl he initially fell in love with.

When you date again, start fresh and follow *The Rules*. Don't interrogate him about what he's been doing since the breakup, and don't ask him when you can get back together now that you've apologized—be light and breezy and end the date first! He has to see you've changed and are easy to be with again! He has to ask you out on more dates and bring up getting back together. You can't!

Be Clear About What You Want

Your *Rules* Weekly Pep Talk

This week, imagine a clear picture of the type of partner you want to be with and what kind of relationship you want to have. Knowing what you don't want in a partner is as important as knowing what you do want. The key is to affirm and make a list of the qualities you are looking for in a partner.

Once you have your list, first focus on finding a partner who has good ethics and motives. Don't date people who are married or unavailable, who won't commit, who have no goals, who show signs of Buyer Beware behavior, or who give lavish gifts to you but at a high price and expect something in return. These are not quality candidates that will make good boyfriends, husbands, or lifelong partners.

If you dated players in the past who used money, bragging, or showing off to impress you, don't let that define your future choices. If you focus on only wealthy people to date, inevitably you get the partner with money, but you may miss out on love, chemistry, and companionship. What if he loses his cushy job or his ex takes him to the cleaners? If you can only have fun in a four-star restaurant or on a yacht, then perhaps you have bigger problems!

BE CLEAR ABOUT WHAT YOU WANT
Daily *Rules*

Day 57: *The Rules* Differ from Other Philosophies
MONDAY

What is your attachment style? Are you avoidant? Secure? Anxious? What is your love language? Is it words of affirmation, acts of service, receiving gifts, quality time, or physical touch? What is your zodiac sign? Your moon? Women like to discuss these things, not just with other women, but with the men they are dating as a way to bond. While there may be some truth to these theories, *The Rules* offer a better way than attachment style, love languages, astrology, tarot card readings, and even therapy! It's about not making the first move! The key is to stay in your power where the world revolves around you, not around them. You do not need to talk to any man first to have your stars align.

Day 58: You Are What You Say
TUESDAY

When women call us for consultations, they often start by saying, "I never meet anyone good," or "I always attract guys who come on strong and then poof," or "I'm a magnet for married or unavailable men." This becomes a self-fulfilling prophecy. You are what you say you are. The truth is, you are not your past. You can, if you want, acknowledge your past, but don't be defined by it or a slave to it. Say, "Now that I am using *The Rules*, I will attract the perfect person I am meant to be with, who fulfills all the wants and needs of the picture I envisioned in my mind and wrote my list about!" Change your thoughts, change your love life!

Day 59: Love Only Those Who Love You

WEDNESDAY

Do you like bad and manipulative playboys? You know, men who love to bomb you with texts but don't follow up with dates? Men who are all talk and no action? Are you bored by men who genuinely like you? Now, we're not saying that you should settle for a man you're not interested in or attracted to. We believe you should feel a spark, but if you're only interested in men who don't want you or who are unavailable or married, then you may want to rethink what kind of person you want to share your life with. If you constantly find fault with men who call you and ask you out, then you either have not met the right dating candidate or you're not giving the nice guys a chance.

Day 60: Not Settling

THURSDAY

The Rules are not just about getting any date. They're about getting a person with a respectable character who will make a faithful boyfriend and future partner. Love may be blind, but Rules Girls are not. So pay attention to your date's behavior. Are they rude to the waiter? Do they stare at the waitress? Do they drink too much? Do they seem annoyed that they drove to your area? Do they get angry easily? What you see is what you get! We call these dates Buyer Beware. If your date is not kind, thoughtful, and well-mannered when they're courting you, then it will only get worse when you're married. Develop clear dating filters!

Day 61: Daddy's Girl
FRIDAY

Maybe you are or were Daddy's girl? This is a wonderful thing, as who doesn't want a kind and loving father? The downside is that you might think that all men are nice and you can say or do anything you want and not get hurt, including calling men, asking them out, and being vulnerable, open, and honest. The fact is, men can be selfish and not emotionally attached, even after they sleep with you. They have no problem never calling again, can break up with you for no good reason (and by text, no less), or can date you for five years and never propose. Whether your father is the salt of the earth or not, you still have to do *The Rules* to ensure you will find a man who falls madly and hopelessly in love with you and doesn't hurt you.

Day 62: Don't Date Resumes
SATURDAY

Some professional women only want to meet professional men, such as doctors or dentists. They refuse to try dating apps or speed-dating events where the men may not be on their socioeconomic level. They say, "No one good goes to those things. I want a very successful guy." We get it. Who doesn't want a successful guy? We understand that if you went to college, he should too; but if you only want dentists, doctors, and lawyers, you might end up alone. Change your definition of a perfect partner. Success is being with someone you are crazy about who is even more crazy about you!

Day 63: Don't Date a Married Man

SUNDAY

If you meet a man, fall in love, and find out he is married, what do you do? Many women give into temptation and tell themselves that it's better to date a married man than to be alone. Don't fool yourself—you are bowing to your *Lower Self* to steal another woman's husband, so you won't get any sympathy from us. Rules Girls do not take or want what is not ours. Empower your *Higher Self* so if a married man asks you out, say, "Call me when you're separated," and have nothing to do with him until then. He will not end his marriage, and you will spend the holidays alone while he takes his wife and kids to Disneyland. No matter how bleak the dating scene is, it's never ever okay to reach out on Facebook to an old high school flame who you know is married to see what he's up to or vice versa. It doesn't matter how much you feel sorry for him because of his alleged miserable wife or life. He is off-limits now. Do not see married men for any reason.

Apply *The Rules* to Achieve Your Higher Self

1 Instead of reading his horoscope, reread *The Rules*!

2 Replace "I've never had any luck in love" with "I attract the best and most loving men."

3 Pay attention to your date's behavior. Does he scream at waiters? Is he asking for your Venmo to split the check?

WEEK TWO

Putting Yourself Out There

Your *Rules* Weekly Pep Talk

This week, consider the law of averages. The more often you put yourself out into the world to meet dating candidates, the more choices you will have and the higher chance you have of meeting your future partner. After all, 90% of life is just showing up! Brenè Brown said, "Sometimes the bravest and most important thing you can do is just show up." How true for single or divorced people looking to fall in love and be married!

No matter how hectic your life is with work, kids, family, and friends, find two or three hours a week to go out wherever you might find potential partners! Choose to dress up and go to a pleasant restaurant or hotel that has a bar with a friend instead of going to the diner in sweatpants with your married BFF. Or go to a church, social event, or a club that is having a singles event. If you have a hobby like bird-watching, attend a bird-watching event. Who knows, you might meet a man or friend who has the same interest. Being seen and presenting a confident version of yourself is everything.

PUTTING YOURSELF OUT THERE
Daily *Rules*

Day 64: Faith without Works
MONDAY

When you begin *The Rules*, you don't have to believe you will meet your dream partner—you just have to take action. Faith is nice but unnecessary to make a choice to go out of your house and put yourself in social situations. Even when you have doubts, you can still go to a bar or singles event with a friend so you don't feel so alone. You will muster a little faith each time you get dressed up and leave the house. You don't have to love yourself completely either to meet your soulmate. Who loves themselves all the time, anyway? You just have to love yourself enough to gather the courage to post a headshot and full-length shot in a light-hearted and breezy profile on several popular dating apps. People who take specific actions and strategize are more likely to succeed than ones who sit in a yoga position and meditate.

Day 65: You Only Need One
TUESDAY

A client followed our advice to go to three singles parties a week to meet Mr. Right, whether or not she felt like it. At one party, there were about twenty women and five men. "Oh no, there's no way I'm going to meet anyone tonight. I might as well go home," she thought. Two minutes later, a man approached her and spoke to her first. Being a Rules Girl, she flitted around the room so he was inspired to follow her. Her strategy worked, and he got her number. They are married now. So don't think, "The odds are stacked against me. It will never happen." Instead think, "I just need to meet one."

Day 66: You Can't Pursue
WEDNESDAY

You can pursue your career and pick your car, your condo, and your cable provider, but we don't recommend you pick or pursue your partner! This is a hard concept for most women to swallow, especially successful ones. Ask an Olympic athlete, CEO, or Instagram influencer to wait for someone else to make the first move, and they will tell you you're crazy or living in the Stone Age. She will say that she didn't become a rowing champion or climb the corporate ladder or amass a million followers to sit around waiting by the phone. She'll say, "I am a woman, hear me roar! Now watch me ask my cute coworker to go out for drinks. I can do anything!" Believe us, we've heard it all and it won't end well. Don't do it!

Day 67: Stop Hiding
THURSDAY

Some women love to reread and even quote *The Rules*. They also take relationship courses and workshops. They join Facebook support groups. They analyze celebrity relationships. But they don't go on very many or any dates. They are more like research analysts than participants.

Needless to say, dating is not a spectator sport. While it's good to know *The Rules,* you also need to get a manicure and blowout and go out on a date or post pretty photos on a dating app over staying at home and highlighting our books. You have to be in it to win it. You can reread *The Rules* in between dates.

Day 68: Dedicated Meetups

FRIDAY

Clients often ask us where to meet men. We suggest that in addition to dating apps they google "singles events," "speed dating," or "meetups" in their area. Some feel reluctant to attend anything so structured, preferring to meet men naturally, such as at a museum or the beach. But we explain that museumgoers and beachgoers may be there to look at paintings or the ocean, not for their soulmates, and that a dedicated singles event will attract more marriage-minded men. Are you resisting meeting men because you don't like the idea of singles events? Get over it!

Day 69: Singles Resort

SATURDAY

When we suggest going to upscale restaurants, bars, or singles vacations like Club Med, some women say they would like to but don't drink or have anyone to go with or they would rather travel to more exotic places like Africa rather than a singles resort. We explain that you don't have to drink alcohol to go to a bar. You can drink water or soda. You don't have to go with someone. You can go alone and infer, *wink, wink*, you are meeting a friend there who doesn't show up. Get real—the chances of meeting a marriage-minded man at a singles resort or bar is greater than meeting a man on a safari in Africa.

Day 70: Practice Makes Perfect

SUNDAY

The more actions you take, the more confident you will become. For example, many women fear ending the date first, but when they do it again and again, they become more confident and less fearful about it. You will see that nothing terrible happens when you say, "This was fun, but I have to get going." Perhaps a guy will look a little shocked that you are ending the date after an hour because he has been spoiled by non–*Rules* Girls actually extending their first date. But, if anything, he'll find it refreshing, as many women never end the date first; rather, they suggest another bar or ask, "So what are we going to do next?" They even suggest sleepovers followed by brunch!

Apply *The Rules* to Achieve Your Higher Self

1   Don't think, "Should I go out or not?" If you're single, just put on a pretty outfit and go! Dating is one area where deliberating can be detrimental. Don't think your way into watching a rom-com on your couch!

2   Go to a singles event, bar, or club, even if there's a low turnout. Remember, you're just looking for one boyfriend and husband, not ten!

3   If you want to meet men, better to go to twenty meetups than one safari to Africa.

If You Want to Be Courted, Don't Take the Lead

Your *Rules* Weekly Pep Talk

This week, accept now that only one person in a relationship can take the lead, especially in courtship. Depending on who is the feminine or masculine partner, most often, the masculine partner should take the lead. If both partners take the lead in the romantic dance, they will trip over each other's feet. We acknowledge most women can run a condo meeting, take the lead on their office's business presentation, or lead their girlfriends on a bachelorette party in a foreign country, but it's not effective to take the lead in their romantic relationships without possibly getting hurt or chasing their dates away.

Moving forward, focus on leading in every area of your life, but step back with your romantic partners and let them lead you and take care of the courtship. This is a gift because your partner will grow more empowered and take pride in taking care of you. Take deep breaths, let go, and practice being whisked around the dance floor and not dragging your partner around. See how you'll become a magnet to a long line of partners who'll want to dance with you for the rest of their lives.

IF YOU WANT TO BE COURTED, DON'T TAKE THE LEAD

Daily *Rules*

Day 71: Setting Boundaries

MONDAY

Consider how many people offer themselves freely, constantly texting, sexting, and jumping into bed. Is this the part you want to play in dating for the rest of your life? It's really okay not to be more proactive or not contact the person you are dating often. You can still genuinely care about the person and show affection, yet use healthy boundaries by limiting calls and texts, turning him down for last-minute dates, not paying for anything, not reciprocating, ending everything first, and not inviting him anywhere. He will dream about you and miss you more.

Day 72: Like a Stop Sign

TUESDAY

Some people feel that *The Rules* are rigid or boring. They heard about *The Rules* in high school or college and thought, "It's not for me." They prefer to *do their own thing* and be their own person or make their own rules. And after a few difficult relationships, they rediscovered *The Rules* and realized that practicing them is not about stifling your spirit, but setting boundaries. *The Rules* are like a stop sign so you don't hurt yourself. Better to be a little boring than hurting.

Day 73: Don't Try Too Hard

WEDNESDAY

Confident girls attract guys who adore them. These girls don't talk too much or try too hard. They naturally feel that they are special and worthy of love. They don't act desperate by chasing guys or dropping everything and everyone to be with men. They are happy with themselves, good listeners, and not nervous wrecks. If you are socially awkward, especially with men, and the type who babbles on a first date, copy women who are chill. Notice how they behave and don't go on and on about themselves and end dates first because they have a fabulous life! *Wink, wink!* "This was fun, thanks, but I have to go. I have a big day tomorrow."

Day 74: Guy Games

THURSDAY

There's a great debate about whether men read relationship books and play their own dating games. We don't think so. But some women are convinced that if they play hard to get, the guy will catch on and play games back by not calling and hoping that the girl will crack and call him. We disagree. We believe that if a guy likes you, he will call you, and if he doesn't like you, he won't. But even if a guy decides to not call you right away to not seem desperate or to get you to call him, it won't work on a Rules Girl! She waits it out. A Rules Girl would rather lose a Saturday night date than lose her self-respect by reaching out. So if he is in fact playing games, her game will be better and last longer than his. If anyone is going to crack, it's him.

Day 75: Do Nothing
FRIDAY

There is nothing you can do to start a relationship. But when you're feeling desperate or delusional, it's easy to believe you can. There are YouTube videos, Insta-experts, and, of course, your own parents telling you "how to subtly approach a guy." You can tell him he's your type and look. You can mention that you're just out of a relationship. You can pretend you're looking for an apartment in his area. You can say you need help with your car or career. Alas, none of these ploys work long term. Showing no interest or very little works best because men want what they can't have.

Day 76: Talk to the Wall
SATURDAY

If there's a cute guy in your group spin class, cooking class, or book club and you're tempted to talk to him first, talk to the other women, talk to the walls, but whatever you do, don't talk to him first. That way, he will know you like him, and you will never know if he liked you. Don't even look at him. Looking is a dead giveaway of interest. Thinking, "I'll talk to him first and then do all the other Rules" is like getting a little pregnant. You can't put the genie back in the bottle. Once he knows you like him because you spoke to him first, you can't undo it. It's better that he thinks you're a little aloof than that you like him!

Day 77: Cheesecake

SUNDAY

One reason we don't contact a guy first is that if you call or text him when he's busy, you might feel hurt when he turns you down or gets off the phone quickly. Some women try it anyway because they're overly confident, love being bold, or are just desperate. One woman invited a guy over to her place to hook up, thinking surely he would be thrilled, but he texted back, "I can't, I'm eating cheesecake." She texted back, "What about after?" and he wrote, "I'm going to be too full from eating cheesecake." Ouch! This is why pursuing men is pointless. When they're interested, they'll contact you! When they're not, you'll get hurt!

Apply *The Rules* to Achieve Your Higher Self

1   Don't listen to well-meaning family members or friends who tell you to call men because it's not the 1950s. Listen to the still small voice inside that tells you that if he likes you, he'll call you, and then get busy doing something else, whether it's calling another Rules Girl or cleaning out your closet.

2   If you're feeling bold, change your hairstyle or redecorate your apartment—don't boldly text a guy you haven't heard from, "Hey, I have two tickets to a comedy club!"

3   If you're bored and tempted to text a guy, read a book or start a book club!

WEEK FOUR
Stepping into Courtship

Your *Rules* Weekly Pep Talk

You have followed *The Rules* for a while and are getting into the groove of dating. This week is extra exciting because it is time to step into courtship. Make this time of exploration and meeting potential partners fun. You now have more time, energy, and money when you are dating because you're not calling, texting, paying for dates, buying gifts, and figuring out ways to "accidentally" run into them to get their attention!

It's great that you can focus on your career, hobbies, family, and friends in addition to dating. This week, focus on giving to yourself and trusting that love follows you when you keep your distance and squeeze them into your world. The less you see him, the more excited you both will be to see each other. He will appreciate the limited time you have together and pay more attention when you're getting to know each other.

STEPPING INTO COURTSHIP
Daily *Rules*

Day 78: We Didn't Want This Either
MONDAY

It might help to know that we didn't want dating to be
this way, either. As feminists and college graduates with
brains and ambition, we thought courtship was equal. We
also thought these Rules sounded crazy. "Dating doesn't
have rules. What's the big deal? Why play games?" But we
realized that the men we didn't pay attention to wouldn't
leave us alone, and the ones we pined over ignored us and
didn't work out. We realized that denying the differences
between the sexes was ineffective, so we finally surrendered
to the fact that this is the way it is, like it or not. Being
rebellious didn't get us anywhere, but being uninterested and
letting men chase us worked.

Day 79: Still Works
TUESDAY

Some women learned about *The Rules* in their teens because
their mothers gave them our book or just told them, "Don't
make it so easy for men. They're hunters and you're the
prize," and "He has to like you more than you like him."
But other women were less fortunate and didn't find out
about *The Rules* until later in life. A decade or two later, they
realized that it doesn't matter what year it is, *The Rules* will
work effectively if used consistently. Those who were initially

skeptical became sold and are now happily living with or married to the person they love.

Day 80: Silly Strategies
WEDNESDAY

Some dating gurus offer strategies on how to approach a guy. They suggest saying, "You look familiar." or "You remind me of my best friend's brother." They suggest you compliment his shirt or hair. They advise you to throw a party for the sole purpose of inviting your crush. They expect you to believe that these obvious tactics will make a man interested. Such ploys might work short-term because what guy wouldn't be flattered or happy to hook up? But long term he will think you're desperate and drop you for the girl he likes, someone who wouldn't flirt or barely notice him—someone he has to work for!

Day 81: No Encouragement
THURSDAY

There is a theory that men need encouragement, that they are not as tough and bulletproof as women think, that they are fragile and don't know how you feel, which is why you have to tell them. We disagree. Even a shy guy will figure out a way to approach you if he is really interested in you, even if it means risking rejection. Every guy will know how you feel when he asks you out: "Yes" means you're interested, "No" means you're not. Guys don't need winks, texts, links, suggestions, emoji, signs, and love languages. They don't need dating books, courses, or support groups—they just need to like you, ask you out, and have you say "Yes" or "No, thanks."

Day 82: No Games

Some men might tell you they don't like to play games and like women who call them. Don't believe them! The same men marry women who don't contact them. What men call "games" is actually dating with boundaries and self-esteem, saying no to last-minute dates, being light and breezy, and ending everything first. If a man asks if you're playing games or doing *The Rules* on him, look surprised and say, "What rules?" If he says "Well, you never call me," say "I'm not a big caller." Don't take his comments as permission to call him a lot or be an open book.

Day 83: No Rules for Men

We've often been asked to write a *Rules* book for men, but men don't need rules. They are simple and will approach or message a girl they think is pretty or is their type. If a girl turns them down and they really like her, they might even ask her out again. Even a bookworm will figure out a way to ask a girl who sparks his attention. A client did a phone detox and didn't respond to her dating app messages for a month, and a guy who answered her profile was not discouraged. He wrote three times, *Hi, I like your profile, would you like to chat sometime?...Hi, it's me again, free for drinks?...Me again! Any chance we can meet?* She finally answered, they met, and now they're married. No one needed to tell him what to do or not to give up.

Day 84: When to Compliment
SUNDAY

Men don't need compliments when they're dating you. They need it when they're married. Thank your husband for taking out the garbage, filling the gas tank, rotating the tires, paying the bills, and anything and everything you can think of. Most married women are not only not complimenting their husbands, they are criticizing them for not making more money or not fixing things around the house. It's your *Lower Self* focusing on what's wrong. What you focus on grows, so if you focus on what you're not getting from your husband, you'll get more of that. If you focus on what you're getting, you'll get more of that! *Higher Self* focuses on the good in every situation!

Apply *The Rules* to Achieve Your Higher Self

1   Whenever you feel mean about not calling men, remind yourself that you're doing them a favor. You're creating longing and making them work for you, which is good for them!

2   When you're tempted to talk to a "shy guy" at a party, talk to a shy girl.

3   Don't ask guys about their love languages, horoscopes, or five-year plans—that makes it so obvious you're interested in them! Talk about work, the weather, TV shows, movies, or sports.

WEEK FIVE
Communicating

Your *Rules* Weekly Pep Talk

French philosopher Blaise Pascal said, "All of humanity's problems stem from man's inability to sit quietly in a room alone." Indeed! Waiting and doing nothing are the hardest things for most women, but that's exactly what is required to catch a guy.

On the *Today Show*, cohosts Hoda Kotb and Jenna Bush Hager did a segment on *The Rules* and agreed that women should be the ones to wait in romantic relationships. "I'm a wait . . . er," quipped Kotb. Indeed, the more you wait and build a strong emotional foundation with yourself, the more interested your partner will be. If you are strong and not easily swayed by someone else, then you are ready to be in a committed relationship.

This week, focus on waiting and doing nothing with men, turning off your phone, sitting on your hands if you have to, and staying busy with your own life! Create a bucket list of fun adventures or goals you want to do alone or with friends. The more you enjoy spending time with yourself and friends, the more empowered you will be! This independent energy will in turn make you more attractive and own your feelings and desires more strongly, so you will be able to communicate what you want and need from a partner.

COMMUNICATING

Daily *Rules*

Day 85: Waiting Game
MONDAY

Women today are movers and shakers. They run companies and marathons. Their boldness is admirable, but it doesn't work with dating. What works with dating is waiting— waiting for the guy to talk to or message you first, waiting for him to ask you out, and waiting to be intimate. When a man asks you out, say, "Sure." Don't say, "Where? When? What time?" Dating is like a chess game. You can't jump ahead by three moves. Don't initiate intimacy to ensure a guy is interested, to see if you're physically compatible, or because you have been celibate for five years and can't wait! Every woman who has done this lived to regret it, so slow down, follow his lead . . . and wait!

Day 86: Ten Reasons Not to Make the First Move
TUESDAY

Today, consider 1. If you make the first move, the person you are interested in will know you like them, and the chase will be over! 2. Remember, masculine dates love a challenge. 3. You'll never know if they would have approached you first, and that will fill you with insecurity. 4. Because you started it, they'll take you for granted. 5. Because he knows you like him, he will act casual or even lazy. 6. He won't make plans in advance or try to impress you. 7. You may not feel special, and it will take him forever to become exclusive, say "I love you," or propose. 8. You will get practical gifts or no gifts instead of romantic gifts. 9. He will forget your birthday and skip Valentine's Day altogether. 10. One day, he might leave you for the person he chose and spoke to first.

Day 87: Shooting Yourself in the Foot
WEDNESDAY

There's a new movement afloat. People on the dating scene believe in taking their best shot. They refuse to be wallflowers. They say, "Shooters gotta shoot!" They believe in pushing against dating norms and biology and asking anyone out, whether it's sliding into someone's DMs or sending a drink to a cute stranger at a bar. And what if their advances are rejected? No problem! They say they take it in stride and even laugh about it. Well, we're not interested in getting rejected and laughing about it—more like crying about it. Taking the initiative with a potential date is not shooting your best shot—it's shooting yourself in the foot!

Day 88: Efficiency Experts
THURSDAY

Most women today are so powerful that they don't even realize they're being aggressive or too eager. Instead of saying, "Sounds good," when a guy asks her out, a career woman might say, "Great, I'm going to be in your area tomorrow, so I can just swing by . . . how's drinks at 7 pm?" Or if a long-distance guy contacts her, she might say, "I've been dying to get away, and I have so many frequent flier miles. How does next week look?" If she gets a promotion, she texts a guy, "Hey, we have to celebrate!" That's still asking a guy out! Of course, most men will gladly go along with these effortless meetups and hookups, but they will eventually find the woman's boldness scary and desperate. Remember, your desire to be efficient, move things along, use your free airline miles, or celebrate can't be more important than the chase!

Day 89: You Can't!

FRIDAY

How do you get a person to go from messaging you on a dating app to asking you out? Once we have reviewed your profile to make sure your photos are normal and pretty (nothing wild and crazy!) and your answers are light and breezy (nothing deep and therapeutic!) there is nothing more you can do. You can't drop hints or suggest anything. Don't say, "Why don't we take this offline?" You can't say, "I prefer to talk on the phone or in person." You can't say, "It would be nice to hear your voice." You can only stop texting him back after four messages, because if he doesn't ask you out after that, he's a time-waster.

Day 90: Don't Answer

SATURDAY

Don't answer online guys who ask what you want to do on the first date or what your ideal date is. Let them figure it out. These guys are lazy or are interviewing you, not asking you out. Remember they have four messages to ask you out, so if you answer at all they will eliminate themselves pretty quickly. Also, how long you are single is none of their business. Many women take these questions literally and answer as if they are in a job interview or on *Jeopardy*. "I've been divorced for ten years and haven't been on a date in three years." That's unflattering and TMI. Say, "Just recently." Don't respond to guys who want more photos. The only photo he can have is your profile picture!

Day 91: Don't Lose Your Soul, Self-Respect, and Dignity

SUNDAY

Many women are just as, or even more, ambitious than men. It's hard for them to grasp being someone who quietly sits back and does nothing. So when you want to date a man, don't suggest activities like tennis or the theater or offer advice (for example, one dermatologist likes to tell her dates their SPF [Sun Protection Factor]). Instead, pause, practice self-control, and come from your *Higher Self*. The same effort or drive that makes women so successful in business will have the opposite effect with men. What benefits a woman in dating is not to lose her soul, self-respect, and dignity by pursuing a man.

Apply *The Rules* to Achieve Your Higher Self

1   When you feel like moving things along with a man ("I'll be in your area next week"), move things along in another area of your life. Finish your taxes, book a colonoscopy, or do something else you're avoiding, like donating clothes you don't wear.

2   If you feel that "shooters gotta shoot," take up a sport like pool or golf!

3   If you find it hard to be patient, take up a game like chess that forces you to wait!

WEEK SIX
Ground Rules for Dating

Your *Rules* Weekly Pep Talk

Knowing and following *The Rules* are two totally different steps, and you have to learn both well in order to eventually succeed at finding your lifelong partner. These secrets are key to reaching success in creating happy and healthy relationships. We believe in you and know you can do it!

When we ask clients, "Who spoke to whom first?" or "Who ended the relationship?" some reply, "Oh, it was mutual." That's impossible! Someone has to speak to someone first, and someone has to initiate the breakup. Trying to pretend that men and women are romantically similar in how they date is delusional and naïve. Men are hunters, and women are gatherers. Men are quiet, hunting out in the forest or playing on the golf course, and women are talkative, even in a yoga class where you're not supposed to talk. Times may be very different, but so many of our innate male and female instincts are still ingrained in us.

This week, focus on the fact that men and women are different—*vive la différence*. Men love a challenge, and that's why playing hard to get really works! He prefers to win you over and not be handed over as a trophy. This week, consider why men making the first move is so important in creating a long-lasting relationship.

GROUND RULES FOR DATING
Daily *Rules*

Day 92: Vive La Différence
MONDAY

While we're feminists, we believe feminism is about equal rights and opportunities, not biology. Biologically, men and women are different. Most men are natural-born hunters. They love a chase—the stock market, sports, and fast cars. Women like security. A woman goes on a first date and calls five girlfriends afterwards to analyze what happened. A guy goes on a first date and then watches a football game. Women who call men, ask them out, travel to men, or pay for dates destroy male instincts and ambition. So when you don't hear from a guy, resist the urge to text, "What's up?" or "I miss you . . . " Stop!

Day 93: Much Ado About Paying
TUESDAY

In the old days, if a guy asked you on a date, he paid and that was the end of it. Now, who pays has become a confusing issue. Some women feel guilty about not paying and immediately pull out their credit cards to let the man know they are financially independent. Other women feel they should at least offer to pay and then secretly hope the guy doesn't take them up on it, so everyone wins. We think the whole splitting the check debate is much ado about nothing. You shouldn't pay, and you shouldn't make an insincere gesture to pay.

The point of a date is courtship and chemistry, not equality or money.

Day 94: Sober Dating
FRIDAY

When you do *The Rules*, you're aware of your *Higher Self* and don't lose yourself in the fog of your *Lower Self.* Do you remember how much you drank and what you did the night before? Women who have more than one drink tend to overshare, get intimate too soon, or even initiate intimacy. If you can't have one drink, then maybe you should have none. You want to be alert on dates so you pace the relationship and know if he's a good guy or not. A Rules Girl doesn't date to kill time, drink champagne, or try interesting appetizers— she's looking for a meaningful relationship and marriage. Are you dating sober or drunk?

Day 95: Reliable!
SATURDAY

A Rules Girl is a reliable girl! She doesn't drop everything to be with a guy. A guy is an add-on to her already full life, not her whole life. Therefore, she doesn't cancel plans with friends or family. "Sorry Michael just called. Can I get a rain check?" And she doesn't skip the gym or her session with her trainer, therapist, or life coach. "I have to reschedule. Michael wants to go to the movies..." She doesn't skip salsa or tennis lessons to accept a last-minute invitation from Michael. "I can't make it because Michael got courtside tickets to a basketball game." She has integrity; her *Higher Self* decides, and her *Lower Self* doesn't get a vote!

Day 96: Not Gold Diggers

FRIDAY

Contrary to what some skeptics think, a Rules Girl is not looking for free meals, four-star restaurants, lots of gifts, or bling. She is looking for love, respect, and to be cherished. She would rather receive a less expensive romantic gift like flowers, candy, or dinner than an expensive practical gift like an iPad for Valentine's Day. It's not the amount of money a man spends that matters, but the type of gift. A forty-year-old client met a forty-five-year-old CEO on a dating app. He bought her a pricey air fryer for Valentine's Day, but he never said "exclusive" or "I love you," even after a year. We told her to ask him his intentions, and if he had none or just wanted to have fun, then we told her to break up with him and go back to dating, which she initially resisted because she loved him. We said, "Unfortunately, he doesn't love you back." She finally listened and was grateful she did because she met a thirty-nine-year-old modest tennis instructor on another dating app who asked to be exclusive and then said "I love you" after six dates. Then he proposed after ten months with his grandmother's ring and a wedding date.

Day 97: Don't See Him Again

SATURDAY

It's the kiss of death if a guy asks you to split the check. If he's thinking about the cost of the Caesar salad and chicken parmesan, then he's not thinking about you and seeing you again. Sometimes a server will ask if you're splitting the check and you will feel obligated to pay. Don't! A respectful guy would never let that happen and would still insist on paying. Otherwise, he just doesn't like you enough, and you're in the friend or friends-with-benefits zone. A guy who pays and then says, "Don't worry, I'll Venmo you," is also not someone you should see again. Better that he takes you to a less expensive restaurant and pays than ever ask you to chip in. Never feel badly for a man paying for dinner or taking you out.

Day 98: Don't Be So Nice

SUNDAY

When we advise our clients not to pay or travel to a man, they argue they're just trying to be "nice." *The Rules* are a truth serum, and the truth is, these women want to be liked way too much in order to get their partner to propose. When the right person likes you, you don't have to be overly nice or try too hard or pay. It's best to be chill, not overjoyed, when he asks you out. Oprah Winfrey famously said over the years that when she thought she was being nice, she was actually people-pleasing because she wanted to be liked. Check your motives!

Apply *The Rules* to Achieve Your Higher Self

1   When you feel guilty about not splitting the check, mentally add up how much you spent on your hair, nails, and clothes. You're more than even!

2   Don't be overjoyed when you get an expensive gadget like an air fryer from your boyfriend for your birthday. Better to get a romantic gift that's less pricey!

3   If you think a relationship is mutual, use *The Rules Dating Journal* or a notebook or your phone to record who is calling whom and who is suggesting what. It's not mutual!

WEEK SEVEN
Getting to Know Your Date

Your *Rules* Weekly Pep Talk

Don't be in a hurry! Your persistence in following *The Rules* will pay off. The only pressure being put on you to hurry and get to the finish line of marriage is YOU! Take off the pressure and enjoy the dating ride. Enjoy getting to know your dates, little by little, and you will practice and become better at dating and a more compassionate person as you learn more about different men's personalities, quirks, and interests.

This week, slow down and realize that it takes time to get to know all the facets of another person, usually four seasons. Pop culture would have you believe in "whirlwind courtships." The truth is that there are time-tested rules that work and trends that don't work. Constant contact by phone and text, frequent trips, investing in a business together, and moving in prematurely kills the chase. Slow and steady wins the race, not being available 24/7 whenever he calls or texts. Trust us, we have seen it repeatedly when a guy gets bored and you get hurt! Too much, too soon is never good, so take your time and enjoy the ride.

GETTING TO KNOW YOUR DATE

Daily *Rules*

Day 99: If You Have to Ask

MONDAY

The beauty of *The Rules* is that when Mr. Right falls for you, he will only have eyes for you! He'll think you're prettier than a supermodel. You will feel secure and never worry that he's a womanizer. But if you did *The Rules* and still suspect that he's cheating, then he could be an incorrigible player. If he's constantly checking his texts, excusing himself to take calls, or acting strangely secretive and never letting his phone out of his sight, he may see other women and is stringing you along. When a woman thinks, "I wonder if my boyfriend is cheating on me," she's either paranoid from past experiences or he probably is. Find out before you proceed further!

Day 100: Don't Force Him to Talk

TUESDAY

Most women love to talk, especially about feelings and the nuances of a relationship—men, not so much. So don't force a guy to discuss Zodiac signs or celebrity couples, watch Hallmark movies, or read relationship books if he's not interested. If anything, you should watch or talk about what he likes, whether it's action-adventure movies, comedy, politics, and football. After all, a man likes your looks and marries you, he wants someone he can be himself with. Don't pressure him to talk a lot. As a famous businessman said, "I work all day. I don't want to work on the relationship when I get home!"

Day 101: Excuses

WEDNESDAY

Don't make up reasons to reach out to a guy. Some women throw Super Bowl parties in order to invite their cute neighbor over who has never shown interest. Some women call a guy when they have car trouble instead of calling AAA. Some women text a guy to ask for career advice instead of talking to a headhunter. None of these strategies work long term. If you invite a guy to your party, he will drink your beer and eat your chips. If you ask for help, he will happily oblige and even sleep with you, but he won't ask you out or want to be in a relationship with you.

Day 102: No Quid Pro Quo

THURSDAY

Some women feel that making plans, paying, and travel-ing to a guy are ways to show him you are not passive, but independent and able to afford an airplane ticket or fancy meal. Other women want to pay their own way so as not to feel sexually obligated. But both demonstrate faulty thinking. You do not have to show or prove anything. You just have to show up. You don't owe your date anything. There is no *quid pro quo* here. It doesn't matter if he bought you dinner, drinks, or flowers—you don't have to pay for anything or sleep with him. Believe that you deserve to be courted properly with no strings attached!

Day 103: No More Vagueness

FRIDAY

Keep track of *The Rules* that are working. If you don't want to be unconscious, write everything down, keep a diary, or use *The Rules Dating Journal* to record who spoke to whom first, who called or texted first, the length of calls and dates, how many drinks you had, if he skipped a week or forgot plans, and who ended everything first so that you know what's going on and are not blindsided if it doesn't work out.

Day 104: Right Reaction

SATURDAY

If you feel rude saying no when a relatively new guy asks you to go away with him for five days or travel to him, stop and ask yourself what your confident friend, coworker, or a Rules Girl would do in this situation. And then do it! Why suffer and make needless mistakes? A confident girl would nonchalantly say, "Sorry, I can't get away," or "Actually, it's better if we meet near me," and see how he reacts. She would not turn herself into a pretzel. Nor would she get angry and say, "I can't believe you are asking me to drive to you!" She does what's good for her but doesn't get huffy or let her tiara fall off! Let him be the prince, and you be the princess.

Day 105: Don't Act So Surprised

SUNDAY

Visualize your dates wining and dining you and sending you flowers all the time! Too many women lacking in self-esteem act overly grateful when a man takes them out. They thank him on the date, and they thank him again in a text the next day. They call him to thank him for the flowers instead of waiting for him to call and ask if the flowers arrived. Similarly, when a man texts them, they get so excited as if they won the lottery and feel compelled to answer immediately, lest he thinks they are rude. You must act like you get texts from men all the time and can barely keep up!

Apply *The Rules* to Achieve Your Higher Self

1   Don't act overly thrilled or gush about getting flowers from a guy. Act like you get flowers all the time or send bouquets to yourself.

2   When you want to call a guy to fix your MacBook, call AppleCare!

3   If you can't remember how long the calls and dates are and who ended them first, use a notebook or *The Rules Dating Journal* to record everything. Don't be unconscious!

WEEK EIGHT
Don't Be Blind to Reality

Your *Rules* Weekly Pep Talk

This week, before you go on any dates, focus on being self-controlled and not oversharing. Instead of blurting out your whole life of woes and gossip, consider writing out a list of what you want to share, in what order, and over what period of time of dating. Do you really want someone you don't know well or trust yet to know the most intimate stories of your life? Think before you share. Your sharing list doesn't have to be complicated—just write down a basic outline of the key highlights of your life you want to share that come from your *Higher Self* and share carefully over a long stretch of time so you don't share too much, too quickly.

Become conscious of how much you talk on dates. It is easy after a couple of drinks to overshare and overwhelm your date with TMI! We are not suggesting you suppress your vivacious personality, but listen more, learn more about your date, and notice any red flags before you share anything about your life. It is a key rule to be a good listener and observer so you can stay rational and weed out Buyer Beware men, such as alcoholics, womanizers, cheapskates, narcissists, and complainers.

This week, focus on what, how much, and when to share; listening more so you can be more discerning about who your date is; and putting your radar up!

DON'T BE BLIND TO REALITY
Daily *Rules*

Day 106: Mixed Messages
MONDAY

Women sometimes complain that a man is giving them mixed messages. "He's really fun on the date, but then I don't hear from him for weeks," or "He says he doesn't want to be in a relationship, but then he asks me to be his plus-one for a wedding," or "He texts a lot but doesn't ask me out." News flash! There are no mixed messages. Men who disappear, who are only interested in a date for a wedding, or who chat you up but don't take you out are not into you. Mixed messages mean NO! Your *Lower Self* might be mixed up, but your *Higher Self* knows these responses are telling you a clear message. This is why listening, being discerning, and watching out for red flags early on when you're dating are so important, so you don't end up with one of these guys.

Day 107: Too Casual
TUESDAY

If the guy you're dating is constantly downgrading plans, for example instead of dinner at a fine restaurant he changes it to hanging out at his place and ordering in; he talks about taking you away for the weekend and then asks you to pay for your plane ticket and half of the hotel; he says, "Let me know when you're available," instead of pinpointing to go out on Saturday night; or if he acts nonchalant instead of excited about celebrating Valentine's Day or your birthday with you, this a case of Buyer Beware. Being casual is a red flag that a guy wants the opposite of courtship, and it rarely ends in a commitment. Next!

Day 108: Low Effort
WEDNESDAY

If you pay attention and listen closely to your date early on, you will notice that Buyer Beware dates put in low effort. They say things like, "Call me when you're free." That's putting the onus on you to pursue them instead of saying, "Can I see you Saturday night?" Or they say, "Do you want to pick the place?" instead of researching special restaurants and making reservations. Or they suggest meeting near them or halfway, which kills courtship, as he should be the one traveling and being inconvenienced, not you. Don't respond to low-effort men. Don't say, "I can't believe you're asking me to find the restaurant." Rules Girls stay in their power, keep calm, and don't argue or whine—they ignore these men and move on!

Day 109: Complainers
THURSDAY

Guys who complain before they even meet you are Buyer Beware. Red flag! For example, some online guys will ask a woman endless questions and not ask her out. Rather than participate in pen-pal conversations, we tell women to stop writing back after four text exchanges. A good guy will get the hint and ask for a date. A Buyer Beware guy will get annoyed or angry and write things like, "Not a big conversationalist, are you?" or "How are we supposed to get to know each other if you don't write more than two words?" He's looking to blame you for his lack of interest. Don't take the bait and don't write back!

Day 110: You're Demoted
FRIDAY

People who date you and sleep with you and then say, "Let's just be friends," are a big red flag and Buyer Beware men. You should not be friends with them. Don't be flattered—you've been demoted. Don't meet for drinks or lunch, and block him on social media. He will waste your time and probably want to use you to talk about other girls he's dating. He may want to sleep with you again "as friends." You need a friend with benefits like a hole in the head. Any relationship that goes from romantic to platonic is dead. Your *Lower Self* might think having an ex around is cool. Your *Higher Self* knows it's a demotion!

Day 111: Break-Up Text
SATURDAY

If a guy breaks up with you, Buyer Beware, he can do it again. Or he can propose and not show up at the wedding, or he can marry you and divorce you. Some men end a relationship by texting, "It's over." Think "Good riddance!" not "How can I get him back?" On the other hand, if you did *The Rules* in the beginning and then became difficult or mean, that may explain why he ended it. Do some soul-searching. Some women can become so nasty via their *Lower Selves* that the guy can't take it. If that's the case, work on being your *Higher Self*. If he finds you difficult, so will other men.

Day 112: Addicts

SUNDAY

Does the guy you are dating drink too much? Does he have a porn addiction? Is he a workaholic? Is he in debt? What you see is what you get! Don't date an alcoholic, drug addict, porn addict, workaholic, gambler, or debtor and then act surprised when he behaves accordingly. He may or may not stop drinking, watching porn, or betting at the racetrack. If you decide to date him, either accept him or look the other way. Don't think that you are going to change him. But if you say, "It's either me or the booze," and he picks you, it's usually because he wanted to stop drinking anyway. Know it will be a challenge and go to Al-Anon to get support.

Apply *The Rules* to Achieve Your Higher Self

1   If a new guy asks you to split the check, say "OK" and never see him again!

2   If an online guy asks a lot of questions (favorite color) but doesn't ask you out, he might be curious but not serious. Next!

3   If your boyfriend breaks up with you but wants to stay friends, say "No thanks" and have nothing to do with him!

WEEK NINE
Take a Deep Breath and Begin Again

Your *Rules* Weekly Pep Talk

If you are reading this book, you may realize how many of your past dating rules are the opposite of *The Rules* we share. Don't worry, because with each new date you go on, you can begin anew. You know now not to initiate relationships, stay with men who show low effort or don't commit, or beat yourself up for dating mistakes. Ruminating about past mistakes is using your *Lower Self.* Learning and not repeating the past is choosing your *Higher Self.*

By using *The Rules Handbook* every day, you are learning and implementing healthy habits and boundaries into your life. This week, we'd like you to focus on doing one or two essential *Rules,* like not texting first or suggesting plans, as opposed to regretting the past and feeling like a failure! There are no failures, just tiny wins after mistakes, that lead you to achieve even bigger successes.

TAKE A DEEP BREATH AND BEGIN AGAIN
Daily *Rules*

Day 113: You Still Have Time to Reset
MONDAY

If you already contacted a guy first, stop contacting him now.
If you already bought him a shirt, don't buy him anything
else. If you already paid for your share of a trip, don't pay
any more or go on any more trips. If you let the dates go on
endlessly or he ended the date first, look at your watch and
end the next date extra early. Whatever *Rules* you broke,
don't break anymore. You don't have to be perfect. You can't
undo the past, but you can become stricter going forward.
If you're seeing him four, five, six or seven nights a week, see
him three times a week. Whatever it is, do less!

Day 114: Not His Mother
TUESDAY

Some women make the mistake of acting like their husband's
mother, constantly critiquing him privately and even
publicly. They tell him what to do and what to eat. They
chide him for talking with his mouth full. They say "I don't
like how you handled that," or "I can't believe you're wearing
that." They are disrespectful or downright rude and then
wonder why their husbands avoid them. Half the time, these
women don't even realize they're being critical. They are
unconscious (*Lower Self*). Compliment your husband or say

nothing (*Higher Self*). You're not his mother, and he's not your project!

Day 115: Don't Tell Men What to Do

WEDNESDAY

Don't tell a person how to date you! Don't say, "I prefer calls to texts, and this is what I need..." We're not telling men what to do—we're observing their behavior and acting accordingly. It's not a victory if a date opens the car door because you tell him to do it. Some people ask their dates to sign contracts stipulating how they should communicate or that they won't fight or cheat. You don't tell your new boss, "I expect a promotion and a corner office." You just do your work and reap your rewards. If you do *The Rules*, you will automatically get courtship. If you act controlling, a date will think you're too much work and move on.

Day 116: Don't Sell Yourself Short

THURSDAY

Are you pouring your heart and soul into your online profile and wondering why it's not working? Are you writing sales-y bios like, "If you're looking for a shoulder to cry on, someone to drive you to the ER when you're sick, or pick you up from the airport after a business trip, then you can count on me. I also make a fantastic chicken parmesan and chocolate layer cake." Sales-y bios will attract users and players, as you're offering to be their therapist, Uber driver, and cook! A *Rules*-y profile is factual and offers nothing: "When I'm not working, I like to exercise, read, and travel . . . " Say and sell less!

Day 117: Wasting Time
FRIDAY

Women waste time with men in so many ways. There are women who hook up with their personal trainer for five years, even though he has a girlfriend and it's never going to be anything. There are forty-plus-year-olds dating guys half their age even though there's no future, and when you ask them why, they say younger guys are more fun and older guys have more baggage. There are women dating men for years who, when asked where this is going, say, "I'm not a commitment-type person." There are women who go straight home after work and don't go out socially. They're dating no one for years or decades! How are you wasting time?

Day 118: Get Busy
SATURDAY

The biggest mistake women make when they meet a new man is to make him their whole life. They drop the gym, friends, and other interests and focus on him. When you meet a new guy is exactly when you should get busy. Maybe take up a sport or start a food Instagram account. You should be so busy buying pretty tennis skirts and working on your serve or going to restaurants and taking interesting photos and videos of appetizers that you barely notice if he's texting

you or not. You're playing pickleball! You are not staring at
your phone!

Day 119: The Date Who Always Cancels
SUNDAY

People who cancel dates more than once, unless it's a bona
fide emergency, are not future partner material. Unless his
mother is in the hospital or someone died, he should want to
be with you. People who cancel because they are slammed
with work or can't find their car keys or got last-minute
tickets to a ball game are not that into you. A person who
truly cares or is in love will take an Uber or borrow a car or
give away tickets to the ball game to see you. How do you
know if the person is telling the truth? People who cancel
and don't reschedule quickly are lying or being polite. You
will probably never see them again! Now some women
argue, "I don't care if a guy cancels because sometimes I
need to cancel too." It's okay if you cancel, but it's not okay
if he cancels. Remember, you're the more sensitive one, the
one reading this how-not-to-get-hurt book, the one who gets
upset, disappointed, or even crushed by cancellations. Your
canceling is not the same. You just spent an hour on hair and
makeup—he combed his hair. But more importantly, his
canceling means he can live without you, so it's not okay if he
cancels. He'll be fine either way, but you won't!

Apply *The Rules* to Achieve Your Higher Self

1   If you broke a rule like accepting a last-minute date, don't feel obligated to keep it. You can cancel! Something came up! You're suddenly busy!

2   If your online profile sounds like a self-help book or poem (looking for my soulmate), rewrite it to simply say what you like to do (work out, go to the beach, etc.) when you're not working.

3   When you meet a guy is exactly when you should take up a hobby so you don't make him your whole world! Tennis anyone?

WEEK TEN

Are You Ready to Strictly Date by *The Rules*?

Your *Rules* Weekly Pep Talk

The Rules are guidelines for successful dating. So we believe, the stricter, the better! We know we can come off direct and to the point, but we know from working with clients for over thirty years that these *Rules* really work! Thousands of women have been successful at finding their lifelong partners and are living happily together.

This week, don't focus on what you might miss out on from your old Wild West days of dating: nonstop texting, oversharing, and marathon dates. Now by doing *The Rules*, you are setting boundaries and building your self-esteem, and you will soon have a boyfriend and future husband. Don't think of *The Rules* as restrictive but as empowering because you are no longer a slave to every *Lower Self* urge to text, see your dates all the time, sleep with them way too soon, and lose yourself in a relationship. When you practice *The Rules*, you keep YOU!

ARE YOU READY TO STRICTLY DATE BY *THE RULES?*
Daily *Rules*

Day 120: Strategy

MONDAY

Is *The Rules* a game? No, because a game suggests trickery and silliness. *The Rules* is a straightforward strategy and serious business for single women who want to have an empowered relationship. It is a dating strategy, a set of dos and don'ts that work. Women who complain that dating is too hard or impossible don't realize or refuse to accept that dating is a strategy—the strategy of not acting desperate no matter how they feel, the strategy of not being an open book, the strategy of controlling their *Lower Self* impulse for instant gratification (calling to hear his voice or hooking up) and holding out for *Higher Self* goals (marriage).

Day 121: By Accident

TUESDAY

Some women claim they didn't do *The Rules* and still got the guy. But when we probe further, we find out that they were getting over their ex and in a bit of a fog and giving off "not looking for anything serious vibes." Not looking for anything serious vibes is exactly *The Rules*, but by accident. Maybe you didn't read the book or set a timer for phone calls or follow *The Rules* "Text-Back Time Chart" in our last book, *Not Your Mother's Rules*—you just didn't care, and that's *The Rules*! When you start caring and wanting to speak to or see him all the time is when you have to be careful and not follow all your feelings but some guidelines!

Day 122: Don't Share You Are Following *The Rules*
WEDNESDAY

We don't recommend you share that you're doing *The Rules* or that you don't call men or sleep with them right away. Why fill him in on your dating strategy? That's like giving your competitor your marketing campaign. It's none of anyone's business. But if you do, don't worry. He probably won't know what you're talking about. If he does, just say you're reading a lot of self-help books lately and this is just one of them. Or, you can feign amnesia or play dumb. "What rules?" In any case, keep not calling him and being busy. What you do is more important than what you say.

Day 123: Plan A versus Plan B
THURSDAY

The very strictness of *The Rules* is what makes them work! If we thought women should call men or talk on the phone for thirty minutes instead of ten minutes, we would have said so. On the contrary, every rule was carefully thought out after years of observing what works and doesn't work in romantic relationships. Our feeling is still that stricter is better if you want results. Most men have been so spoiled over the years by women chasing them or being too available that we have to "un-spoil" them. But if you don't want to be so strict, just do less or Plan B!

Day 124: Dead Zone

FRIDAY

If a guy doesn't ask you out by Wednesday for Saturday night, then he doesn't get to talk to you over the weekend, hence the dead-zone-no-contact from Friday night to Monday morning. Some women wonder if the dead zone applies to exclusive relationships. That begs the question, if you're in an exclusive relationship, why aren't you seeing him on the weekends? Is he a doctor on call? Is he a DJ at a club? If you're not together on the weekends for a good reason, you can briefly text back *Crazy busy!* if he texts or calls. In general, if he's busy, you're busier!

Day 125: Popcorn

SATURDAY

A male relationship expert has suggested that if a guy takes you out for dinner and a movie, the least you could do is pay for the popcorn. Buying the popcorn will tell him you are not using him and that you're trying to be fair. Of course, we disagree! If a guy feels taken advantage of because you're not shelling out ten dollars, then he's just not that into you or has abnormal parity or money issues. A guy who likes you won't think about the price of anything. He'll be thinking about how he can hold your hand or put his arms around you during the movie. Don't be fooled by ineffective advice from men!

Day 126: Holidays
SUNDAY

Like Valentine's Day and your birthday, Christmas,
Hanukkah, and New Year's are dates that Mr. Right will not
skip. On the contrary, he will make a big deal about these
occasions and ask you out at least two weeks in advance for
dinner or a family or work party and buy you a gift. You
don't have to remind him or throw a party to get him to
spend time with you. You won't have to drag him under the
mistletoe to trick him into kissing you. Don't ask, "So what
are we doing for the holidays?" If he hasn't brought it up,
make other plans and consider dating others unless he hates
the holidays and you do too.

Apply *The Rules* to Achieve Your Higher Self

1   When you're tempted to listen to relationship gurus who say you can do anything you want, think about what works as opposed to what sounds good!

2   If you accidentally told a guy you're doing *The Rules*, don't mention it again. You read a lot of self-help books. This is just another. No big deal!

3   If you find *The Rules* too strict (ten-minute phone calls), then stay on the phone for fifteen to twenty minutes, but never for hours!

COURSE 3

Empowered
Dating

10 WEEKS

The Rules are not just about dating, but for every area of your life. When we do phone consultations, we ask clients about their family of origin; current relationship and work challenges; their diet and exercise habits; what they believe and don't believe is possible for themselves; their faith, goals, and dreams; and what they like to do in their free time.

The more we know about what makes the client tick, the more we can help her become her best self, her *Higher Self* instead of her *Lower Self*. When a client makes negative or self-defeating comments like, "I'm terrible with men," "I hate online dating!" or "I don't have time to go to bars, the gym, hike, or take up a social sport like tennis," we advise her to change her limiting belief system.

Believing you can do something starts in your mind. It's mind over matter in most cases, as long as it's followed up by action. Believing you can get married, lose weight, get fit, take up hobbies, enjoy life, and get out of your rut is essential for change. The same self-control that goes into not calling or texting men can apply to going to the gym, getting organized, and getting a promotion and all the things you want for yourself. Why be alone when you can have a loving partner? Why be unhealthy when you can be fit? Why live in chaos when you can be organized? Only when you decide you want to get married and be fit, successful, and organized will your actions match your goals. Women who say one thing and do another won't get results. Pump yourself up, but also move your muscles.

WEEK ONE
Relax and Be Yourself

Your *Rules* Weekly Pep Talk

You don't have to be perfect to be loved, cherished, and respected! There is a love match out there in the world for everyone. The more you relax and go with the flow of dating and meeting potential dates, the more chances you will find someone to share your life with you. You just have to do the best you can and let your *Higher Self* lead you on this exciting dating journey.

Some people wonder, "Are *The Rules* about playing hard to get?" When you are ambivalent in your dating life, you may seem like you are "playing hard to get," but you're "being hard to get." You say to-MAY-to,, I say to-MAH-to,! The truth is, you're being hard to get when you have self-esteem, are busy, and have a lot going on! You're playing hard to get when you are insecure.

This week, focus on accepting yourself as you are and not letting these philosophical debates deter you from practicing *The Rules*! It is time to go out into the world and shine so that your soulmate falls in love with you!

RELAX AND BE YOURSELF
Daily *Rules*

Day 127: Good Enough
MONDAY

You don't have to be perfect to date! Many women feel inadequate: too short or too tall, too young or too old, not at goal weight, unemployed, depressed or damaged, busy, newly single or divorced, or fill-in-the-blank to date. They say, "I need to get my finances in order first," or "I need to love myself first," or "I need to get in shape before I get into a relationship!" Sometimes friends or therapists suggest you take a year off from dating to do inner work. We disagree. The best time to date is now. We advise women to find themselves, do yoga, and have fun with friends in addition to dating.

Day 128: Anxiety Reduction
TUESDAY

Let's face it, dating can be anxiety-producing for most women. Does he like me? Will I ever hear from him again? Do we have a date for this weekend? Is he dating anyone else? With *The Rules*, you know exactly where you stand. If you don't hear from him by Wednesday for Saturday night, he's not interested and you make other plans. You're not a nervous wreck waiting until Saturday afternoon or Saturday night to find out. Nor do you shoot him a text to ask, "What's up for the weekend?" or "I thought we had a connection." You have standards and self-esteem—you're not thirsty!

Day 129: Stay in Your Power

WEDNESDAY

Whether you do *The Rules* perfectly, sometimes, or once in a while, try to capture *The Rules'* attitude when you are on your dating journey. So if you make a mistake by hooking up or being overly aggressive or talkative on the first date, end the date first and act nonchalant, not clingy, and don't ask when you are going to see him again. Adjust and spend more time with friends. If you have two tickets to a show, take your mother or your friend, not a new guy. If you've gotten into the bad habit of texting him a lot lately, text less and make sure you write fewer words than him. Literally count the number of words in his text, "How's work going?" That's three words. Therefore, respond with one word, "Good!" If you're always the one hugging him first, wait for him to hug you. It won't be easy, but we have faith you can do it!

Day 130: You're Still You

THURSDAY

There is a reason why *The Rules* are about not pursuing men or being too available. It's not about pretending to be someone else or changing your essence. If you love fashion and traveling and your Instagram account reflects that, don't think you have to delete those photos to date a guy who is more down-to-earth. He either likes you with your penchant for Chanel bags and Eiffel Tower poses or he doesn't. If he thinks you're high-maintenance, then he's not for you. A supermodel, influencer, or bestselling author cannot hide her identity. He can Google it. You want a loving person who likes whoever you are!

Day 131: Follow the Formula

FRIDAY

You don't have to be the prettiest or the smartest girl to catch a guy—you just have to follow *The Rules*. When you are being hard to get and not jumping over hoops to please your date, you are a challenge to win, so be a challenge. Don't call or text men first, and don't ask them out. *The Rules* are a way of acting around dates that makes them more interested and even obsessed with you. We believe in the natural order of things; it goes back to the cave-dweller period, which is that love works best when men pursue women.

Day 132: Being versus Playing

SATURDAY

A celebrity talk show host who interviewed us said she believed in "being" hard to get, not "playing" hard to get. That makes sense when you're genuinely busy, but what if you're unemployed or broke your leg and have all the time in the world? Then we believe you should at least take on a Rules Girl persona and not be so available. So, for example, if a date asks you out for the same night and you have nothing going on, you still have to say, "No, I'm not available," because it's last minute whether or not you have plans. If they ask you to go on a weeklong trip, you still have to say "I'm not able to get away," even though you can. You have a life and can't drop everything you are doing or not doing just because someone asks you to!

Day 133: No Fear of Missing Out

SUNDAY

When you genuinely like yourself, are led by your *Higher Self,* and operate in faith, you are in your power. Your power is limited when you are led by your *Lower Self* and you experience anxiety, scarcity, and low self-worth. *Fear of Missing Out* refers to the feeling that everyone is having more fun than you. FOMO is when you compare yourself to everyone on social media, where everyone seems to have picture-perfect relationships, vacations, walks with their dogs, and other breathtaking thoughts and experiences. Why engage in something that makes you feel bad? It is a form of self-sabotage and insanity. Don't follow or hunt down people on social media because it will encourage your *Lower Self* feelings such as envy and self-pity. Follow your *Higher Self,* not FOMO!

Apply *The Rules* to Achieve Your Higher Self

1   When you think about whether you're going to hear from a guy, think about what you really need to do at that moment (work, laundry, exercise) and do it!

2   If someone wants to debate whether *The Rules* is a game or not, run the other way! It's hard enough to do *The Rules*—don't make it harder by talking to naysayers.

3   Try not to post too much on social media so that he doesn't know everything about you so easily. Mystery, mystery! He has to ask you out to find out more!

WEEK TWO
Create a Dating Plan

Your *Rules* Weekly Pep Talk

This week, create an effective dating plan that will help you define and discover your perfect partner. No one wants to believe that dating is similar to researching and picking the right college or job to apply to, but it is! Write down five or ten nonnegotiables about what your dream partner's characteristics and qualities are that are important to you.

Our sincere intention is to help you walk into the sunset with your perfect partner with your vision of what you want, along with the guidance of *The Rules*. If you know what you want and set boundaries for yourself, this will protect you from getting hurt and finding the person you want to spend the rest of your life with.

The Rules are for your protection and will prevent you from making unnecessary mistakes. This week, make your list, envision what kind of person you want to date, and focus on protecting your heart by creating better boundaries!

CREATE A DATING PLAN

Daily *Rules*

Day 134: Bad Advice

MONDAY

A lot of dating advice sounds good, but we believe it isn't. A dating app a client told us about claims to empower women by telling them to message guys first, a relationship expert suggests flirting with and complimenting men to get their attention, and a therapist encourages a patient to tell her male friend she has a crush on him. These strategies don't work because they are an attempt to circumvent the natural order of things. Making the first move might seem fun in the beginning but invariably ends badly. You can't make a man notice or want you. You can only look your best, hope you're his type, and keep him interested by doing *The Rules*.

Day 135: Spontaneity

TUESDAY

You might think, isn't dating supposed to be more spontaneous? That's only because you're used to being impulsive, calling and texting and FaceTiming, having marathon dates, getting intimate too quickly, and instant gratification. So waiting and pausing and ending things first are going to be hard for you. Your *Lower Self* loves a first date that never ends, an instant connection, and sharing your life story. Your *Higher Self* knows that you should end the date first, wait to be intimate, and pace the relationship for it to last. Who are you going to listen to—that small voice that tells you the truth or your loud, obsessive urges that always lead you astray?

Day 136: For You, Not Everyone
WEDNESDAY

A client asked us, "If everyone does *The Rules* on everyone, there would be no relationships, right?" Wrong. The only people who need to do *The Rules* are those who are searching for effective new ways to find a healthy and loving relationship. Some people are naturally confident and move on quickly when a relationship ends. They may not need strict guidelines to navigate relationships. But if you're sensitive and/or unique, and find it hard to know when to reach out and when to pull back, *The Rules* will give you healthy boundaries and prevent unnecessary hurt.

Day 137: Don't Bother
THURSDAY

How do you get a guy to notice you and ask you out? If you have to ask that question, then he doesn't like you. The short answer is you can't. You can't sit or stand next to him, ask him a question, or make anything happen. He has to notice you and speak to you first. The average guy who walks into a room knows in five seconds which girl he thinks is his type. So staring at him or walking in front of him won't do anything. Many women tell us they wished they knew *The Rules* in college. It would have saved them years of standing next to guys who didn't like them or helping other uninterested guys with their homework and term papers.

Day 138: Jumping through Hoops
FRIDAY

Some women complain *The Rules* are too strict on men because it's asking them to jump through so many hoops. He has to call, he has to find the restaurant, he has to travel, and he has to pay. We explain that making men jump through hoops is good for them because they love jumping through hoops. It's why they play basketball! We remind them they're not just looking for a date or dinner conversation but for a man who goes the distance, a soulmate. They're looking for someone who will be there for them in the delivery room, the emergency room, and the nursing home!

Day 139: Let It Die
SATURDAY

You go on a first one-hour coffee date after work, and he texts you an hour later at 8 pm that he had a nice time and asks about meeting up again. You say, "Sure!" So far, so good. But then his next text at 9 pm is not about the next date—it's "So what are you doing now?" Ignore—it's none of his business what you're doing now. Then his next text is, "Maybe we could hang out tomorrow?" You text back, "Sorry, I already have plans," because it's a last-minute request. Then he writes, "OK, but it would be nice if you made some effort as well..." Don't write back. It's over. You don't have to make any effort. He just had to ask you out in advance . . . or not. Don't keep the conversation going. He's telling you he's difficult. Just let it die. Not all good first dates go anywhere.

Day 140: Intimidated or Not Interested?

SUNDAY

Are some men too intimidated to date certain women? We often hear women claim they are such beautiful models and actresses or successful, rich CEOS, VIPs, and trust fund babies that men are too intimidated to date them. We disagree. We think when a man says a woman is intimidating, what he's really saying is he's not interested and blaming her so he doesn't seem like the bad guy. A man will date and marry a woman who is his type if he is attracted to her, regardless of her looks or bank statement. But if you feel you are seeming unapproachable, perhaps think about dressing more like the girl next door than a Milan fashion model. Men want to marry pretty women with souls, not women who are overly made up, materialistic, or body image junkies.

Apply *The Rules* to Achieve Your Higher Self

1   If anyone—a family member, friend, or even dating coach—tells you to contact a guy first for any reason, run the other way!

2   When you're having fun and not wanting the date to end, look at your watch and say, "Wow, I really have to get going!" Leave him wanting more!

3   Grill happily married women who claim they didn't do *The Rules*. They were probably busy or not initially interested in their future husbands at the time. We call this "*The Rules* by accident."

WEEK THREE
Showing Up

Your *Rules* Weekly Pep Talk

You will not meet any potential dates hiding in your house or dressed in baggy sweatpants! You have to go out into the world and become visible, whether it's on dating apps or at in-person events like speed dating, singles hiking, sports bars, clubs, upscale restaurants, or the gym. You can't hide and expect to meet the love of your life!

This week, focus on scheduling three dating meetups you can go to for an hour each. You can do anything for one hour, right? We understand that for some people it will be easy, but for others, this effort will be really hard. Have courage and take baby steps. Step outside into the dating world as your most empowered self and wear the outfit you feel the most beautiful in.

When you go out on these three dating adventures, consider how you will know if someone is interested in asking you out or how much you should talk or reveal to the other person. Follow *The Rules*.

SHOWING UP
Daily *Rules*

Day 141: How Will They Know?

How does someone know you like them? Simple! You say
yes to dates, you respond to some but not all texts (preferably
date-related texts), you show up, you smile, you laugh at their
jokes, and you're easy to be with. That's it! You don't have to
do more. You don't have to ask, "How do you feel about your
brother not calling you on your birthday?" or "What's your
five-year plan?" You don't have to bake him cookies or pick
him up from the airport or buy him a tie for his job interview. You're not his parent, therapist, or life coach, only his
romantic partner.

Day 142: Quiet, Not Mute

Some women think that when we said don't talk too much on
the first few dates, that we meant for them to be mute. Not
so! While we believe that it's best for the guy to do most of
the talking, you can answer questions or talk about general
topics like work, restaurants, and hobbies. Stay away from
serious subjects like illnesses and relationships. The first is
a downer and the latter is a dead giveaway of interest. If he
talks about his ex, you can say "Wow, that's interesting," or
"Sorry to hear that." We said don't talk too much because
most women have an intense need to communicate and tend

to overshare, and men can find it overwhelming or boring. If you're shy and not a big talker, you won't have a problem. But most women on dates talk too much.

Day 143: Charm School

WEDNESDAY

You can recite *The Rules* backwards and forwards, but you're still not getting dates! Maybe the problem isn't calling or texting, maybe the problem is you! When we wrote *The Rules*, we thought we covered it all. But during private consultations, we realized many women were missing a certain femininity and refinement. They could travel all over the world, speak five languages, and use every feature on their iPhone, but they behaved like corporate raiders. They were pushy, negative, argumentative, vindictive, impatient, or entitled. We realized they might need a little help, so we created a Charm School Online Course.

Day 144: First Move

THURSDAY

When a client asks for advice, the first question we ask is who spoke to whom first. If she spoke to him or messaged him first on an app, it's usually over. Sometimes she just beat him to the punch and the relationship still works out, but it's very rare. If he contacted her first and she broke some rules, such as seeing him too much, she can pull back. But she can't undo the beginning. She can't change the fact that she reached out first. So if you are even thinking about making the first move, don't! Down the road, he might skip weeks or forget your birthday or act noncommittal, and you will wonder why. We know exactly why. You made the first move!

Day 145: Too Soon to Tell

FRIDAY

You had perfect first and second dates. There was chemistry and the conversation just flowed. He invited you to be his plus-one at his friend's wedding. He mentioned that his parents have been married for forty years. You feel you're done dating, that he's Mr. Right. But then he suggests hanging out at his place for the third date, you say, "Thanks, but I'd prefer to go out," and after you set your boundary, you never hear from him again. You're devastated! The reality is, he either just wanted to hook up or met someone else. It's nothing until you've had several consecutive Saturday night dates and exclusivity. Pretend you never met him!

Day 146: Social Media Madness

SATURDAY

Whether you're on Facebook, Instagram, or TikTok, it's easy to reveal too much about your personality and every move you make. Social media is about instant and effortless connections, while *The Rules* are about intrigue and mystery. Don't be flattered by a guy viewing your story (he's viewing many stories) or even a guy who is DMing you to meet up because you're in the same area. It's nothing until he asks you out on a proper date several days in advance, and not because it's convenient. A guy messaged a woman while he was on vacation in her city. She saw him the next day and, every day for six days, drove him around tourist spots and let him stay at her place until he flew back home. She slept with him and was smitten. He contacted her sporadically after that, "Thanks for all your hospitality. I hope I didn't turn you into a hotel and Uber driver LOL!" But he never asked to meet again. It just fizzled, and she was devastated. She was planning the wedding, while he was planning another trip to another city to hook up with another girl. There was no challenge or intrigue for him.

Day 147: Dating a VIP

SUNDAY

If you are dating a VIP or executive, don't act like a groupie. Don't be so impressed by their fame or fortune, and don't accept a date in their city, even if they send a stretch limo or a private plane to pick you up. You're the prize, so they travel to you. No matter how busy they are, you're even busier. VIPs secretly want the girl who doesn't notice them or know who they are. They are so used to women throwing themselves at them that they find a Rules Girl refreshing! A client noticed a popular DJ at the club where she was a cocktail waitress. Having read our chapter, *The Rules for Dating Celebrities*, she glanced away. From the corner of her eye, she noticed other women talking to him first and giving him their phone numbers. While she was busy serving her customers' drinks, he stopped by and asked for her number. They've now been married for twenty-plus years and have three children.

Apply *The Rules* to Achieve Your Higher Self

1 If you can't find a friend to go to a singles event with, go by yourself. Circle the room for an hour and go home.

2 Don't talk about a guy unless you've had three or more consecutive Saturday night dates. It's nothing until at least three dates!

3 If you're not getting second dates, maybe it's not your looks, maybe it's you! Do some soul-searching! Are you argumentative, entitled, or more interested in finance than romance?

WEEK FOUR
Communication Dating Strategy

Your *Rules* Weekly Pep Talk

Do you feel rude not returning men's texts in nanoseconds? Do you think, "Everyone's glued to their phones, and he knows I read his text. He's going to think I'm cold or playing games"? We promise, if you take our *Rules* communication advice and be slow and steady to respond, you will keep the mystery and intrigue going. It is really okay to wait twenty-four hours to respond to a call, text, or email.

Men have no problem ignoring a woman's many texts (plural) while they watch a ball game, go on a Saturday night adventure with their buddies, or get caught up at work. For most men, they are self-focused and live in the moment. They are not ruminating about you every second or worrying about when the next date will be. They will get to it after the game or tomorrow. Nothing is an emergency for a man like it is for a woman.

This week, focus on not worrying what men think about you not responding sooner. They're not! When he calls, texts, or emails, reply with a short and direct response. When you are with him on your next date, be charming, shine your beautiful smile, and be genuinely interested in him. And all those brief communications won't matter!

COMMUNICATION DATING STRATEGY
Daily *Rules*

Day 148: Not for Everyone
MONDAY

The Rules may not be for everyone, but that does not mean the advice is not effective. This time-tested advice really works. You might think, "I can't believe what I'm reading. I run a company, I ran a marathon, I'm on my condo board, and I can't believe I can't call a man I like and ask him out . . . That's crazy." We get it. *The Rules* are not for everyone. They are for women who used to pursue men or were too available and got burned. And if you're okay when a guy doesn't call after you sleep with him or disappears for weeks, bravo. But often, many women feel hurt and get depressed when they don't hear from their date. And *The Rules* can work for them.

Day 149: Practical
TUESDAY

The Rules are practical. We're looking for results. If we're not going to make the first move, text a guy first, sleep with him too soon, not go on a trip, and let him end everything first, we need a payoff. The payoff is that he will fall in love with you; want to see you more, not less; make you feel special; and marry you. He will never feel he is being forced to be in the relationship. He will never say he wants more space or that he feels trapped. On the contrary, he'll say, "I'm the lucky one!" and "What do you want to do this weekend—dinner and a show?"

Day 150: Substitution Method

WEDNESDAY

Some women feel *The Rules* make them passive, no calling or texting or asking men out, no traveling to him or paying, no inviting him to their office party or friend's wedding. A lot of NOs! But while you're not doing all of the above, you're not sitting around doing nothing either. You are busy working, working out, seeing your friends and family, and pursuing hobbies and interests. So when the urge to suggest to a guy "I have two tickets to a show" or "Let's go to a museum" creeps into your mind, call your mother or a friend and take them to the show!

Day 151: Like a Hot Stove

THURSDAY

When you feel the urge to call or text a guy first, think DANGER, DANGER, DANGER! It should feel like touching a hot stove or running into oncoming traffic. Calling a guy first is a bad idea for so many reasons. One, he will know you like him and not think of you as anything special. Two, he might be in the middle of work or watching a ball game, sound disinterested or distracted, and get off the phone first, which might make you feel hurt. Three, he might expect you to call him regularly. Why take a chance?

Why set a precedent for being the pursuer and the more interested party?

Day 152: Too Much Information!

FRIDAY

If a guy asks you how online dating is going, say, "Great!" Don't tell him how hard it is or how there are no good men around. One woman talked so much about her failed relationships and disappointments that her date said, "It sounds like you've been hurt a lot," to which she replied, "Yes, I have." She felt it was necessary to be truthful. We said TMI! No man needs to know how much you've suffered. As far as he's concerned, you've never been hurt, even though you have. You act like the prom queen, even though you weren't. And every man you dated adored you because you deserved it. You wouldn't tell a prospective employer that you're not a great employee at your previous jobs or didn't get along with your coworkers.

Day 153: Holy Grail

SATURDAY

A guy should ask you out by Wednesday for Saturday night during a normal week but several weeks in advance for Valentine's Day. V Day is the holy grail of holidays for a Rules Girl. Any man who skips celebrating his beloved on this day is not in love with you. If he asks at the last minute, it's not such a good sign either. A man in love will make reservations at a special restaurant two weeks or a month in advance. If he forgets the holiday, pretend you forgot it too; if he says Valentine's Day is nothing more than a marketing gimmick, don't argue, but just know he's not Mr. Right.

Day 154: Not Living on the Edge

SUNDAY

If a guy calls too late in the week, such as Friday, for Saturday night, say, "Sorry, I already made plans." Don't add, "But I'm free next Friday." He has to ask for another date. Don't help him date you or make it easy for him by giving him other options. Don't feel guilty about turning him down, either. By saying no to last-minute dates, you are silently training him to ask you out in advance. Rules Girls don't live on the edge, waiting to see what their weekend is going to look like the day before. It's by Wednesday for Saturday or nada. He will ask you sooner if he can't see you at the last minute.

Apply *The Rules* to Achieve Your Higher Self

1   Remember that a *Rules* relationship is not based on the volume of calls, texts, dates, and trips. Just the opposite! *Rules* relationships thrive on mystery and "absence makes the heart grow fonder." It's always "less is more" to catch a man!

2   If the guy you're dating doesn't make holiday plans two weeks in advance, make other plans. Serious guys take Christmas (or Hanukkah) and New Year's Eve seriously!

3   If you haven't heard from a guy by Wednesday at 9 pm, make other plans for Saturday night!

WEEK FIVE

Being Obsessive Will Not Serve You

Your *Rules* Weekly Pep Talk

We understand it's in our nature to go boy crazy, from our first crush on the kindergarten playground to our first high school sweetheart to our whirlwind college romance. If you're like most women, you become easily obsessed when you see a cute guy. After meeting him, do you call five friends to tell them you think he's The One? And when he doesn't ask you out or it doesn't work out for whatever reason, are you devastated? Maybe it is time to stop this vicious roller-coaster ride of romanticizing, getting your hopes up, and then spiraling downwards.

This week, try this: Don't think or talk about him at all until after the third date! It's a fantasy until you have at least three or four consecutive Saturday night dates with him or any guy. Can you imagine a man calling his friends after a first or second date? Men who go home after a date watch ESPN or work! In other words, chill out and wait until the third or fourth date to see what happens!

BEING OBSESSIVE WILL NOT SERVE YOU
Daily *Rules*

Day 155: Wait to Share or Post
MONDAY

Many women are quick to share and post that they are "in a relationship" or "dating" on Facebook and Instagram. They plaster photos of their new boyfriend *ad nauseum* after only one date. "Our first brunch together." Three dates later, "Our one-month anniversary." Follow *The Rules* that only he should post your relationship status first and you should rarely post anything. Sadly, many of these relationships don't last, and it's embarrassing to have to delete posts. Be humble! Wait until you're engaged to tell the world. You don't post that you're going on job interviews; you post that you were hired. Ditto for dating!

Day 156: Being Passive
TUESDAY

You might be thinking, "I'm a lawyer, doctor, MBA, and I'm used to going after what I want and spilling the tea about everything. And I find it hard to sit by the phone waiting for a guy to call." Maybe you are tired of being asked out by men you don't like, so you want to pick. Unfortunately, you can only choose from the pool of men who pick you. But doing *The Rules* is not being passive. You are taking action by showing up to parties and posting your profile on dating apps and saying no to last-minute dates or hookups. You are just not initiating anything because it doesn't work. You're not waiting by the phone—you're living, classy and reserved!

Day 157: Texting Temptation

WEDNESDAY

It's hard not to text back quickly when you're always on your phone, especially after your first few dates. It's like an extension of your hand, so try to put it in your pocketbook for an hour or two while you're working or out with friends and turn it off late at night so you're less likely to text back in nanoseconds at midnight. Writing back quickly will make you look desperate, like you have nothing going on but him. We told a client to wait until the next day to text back a man she just met. By "next day," we meant something normal, like 10 am or noon! She texted back when she woke up at 6 am! We said, "No, that looks like he was the first thing on your mind LOL. Next time wait until at least 10 am!"

Day 158: Don't Overthink

THURSDAY

Do you obsess about what social actions to take to meet men? Singles tennis or singles skiing? Speed dating or a holiday party? An event that is supposed to get thirty people in your area versus fifty people an hour away or stay home and answer your dating app messages? Some women think so much about what to do and end up doing nothing. The answer is, do anything! You never know where you're going to meet your future husband, so just do something. You don't send one resume when you're job-hunting. You send one hundred. Ditto for dating. Pretend your house is on fire and run out the door—go have fun anywhere!

Day 159: Stay Away
FRIDAY

Many women contact us after a great first date. They feel he is The One and want to get off their dating apps and look up his astrological sign. We caution them to calm down, to not even mention his name, because it takes at least three consecutive Saturday night dates to know if a guy is serious about you. Sometimes a guy will drop off the face of the earth after a great first date and you're devastated. Don't be—it's too soon to be too invested. You're either not the woman of his dreams or he met someone else or got back with his ex. It's like a three-round job interview. He's a stranger until after the third or fourth date!

Day 160: Don't Be Tempted
SATURDAY

If your internet is down, don't use that as an excuse to crash at your boyfriend's place. Find a Starbucks or stay with a friend. A woman moved in with her boyfriend to use his Wi-Fi. A neat freak, she told him his place was a mess and moved everything around without his permission. He said she could leave if she didn't like it. She was offended and told him so. We said you can't move in, act like Marie Kondo, complain, and expect him to thank you or be happy about it.

You wouldn't tell your friend she's a slob and move her things around without her permission. We told her to apologize and move out. She did, and they are now happily dating again.

Day 161: Let Go!

SUNDAY

Do you ever wonder if your boyfriend or husband is cheating? Do you regularly check his phone to see if he is texting other women or if his profile is on a dating app? If so, how would you like to have a worry-free relationship with a man you can trust? You can! When you play hard to get, a man feels like he is dating the prom queen. He worked so hard to get you that he doesn't take you for granted. He calls you when he gets a haircut, he calls you when he fills up the tank with gas, and he always makes dinner reservations. He doesn't leave you alone, so he's certainly not cheating.

Apply *The Rules* to Achieve Your Higher Self

1   If you're the type who gets carried away when you meet a cute guy, resist the urge to look him up on social media or ask mutual friends his astrological sign or dating history. None of your business! Do whatever you would do if you had never met him!

2   Don't waste your time and energy until he says "exclusive." Even if you're in a relationship, don't go crazy posting a lot on social media about the two of you. Post about causes you're passionate about, like your 5K run or climate change or anything else!

3   If your car or computer breaks down, don't call the guy you're dating. Call anyone but him to fix it. Women who call a guy for this or that broken thing end up calling him all the time for everything!

WEEK SIX
Ready to Date?

Your *Rules* Weekly Pep Talk

What person these days is not reading self-help books to improve their lives and relationships? After a lot of self-reflection and sometimes therapy, we discover ways to live healthy and more empowered lives. One challenge a lot of our clients face is codependency. They form or maintain unhealthy relationships that are one-sided on their part and enable the people in their lives to have destructive behaviors. They are the ultimate people fixer-uppers!

Codependence is the kiss of death when you are dating! When you meet a man, resist the urge to fix his problems or even suggest anything like a diet, exercise, or a self-help book. Don't go into business together as some couples do when they're dating, which sounds smart but is really dumb because if the relationship ends, you're stuck with an ex for a business partner.

This week, focus on being independent and not giving advice or investing financially in anything together. When you allow the people in your life to fail, experience pain, or step up the plate to care for themselves, you are empowering them and yourself by maintaining your power.

Daily Rules

Day 162: Give Him Nothing
MONDAY

When you're dating, don't give a man anything but you.
Don't give him business connections, medical or legal or
financial advice, or links to interesting articles. He gets
nothing—he only gets you. Women who give too much, who
volunteer to dog sit or help a man with his career or pay his
car insurance, may be genuinely nice or may want love in
return. Either way, it's a big mistake to give anything. You
will only attract users. Women are natural caretakers. They
will drop everything to take a man to the ER or to bail him
out of jail. Bad idea!

Day 163: Splitting the Check
TUESDAY

Splitting the check is fine for coworkers, but not for courtship.
Tell yourself it's his pleasure to pick up the tab. It's a small
price to pay to be with you, so don't feel guilty. You're
gracing him with your presence. But if you feel awkward
about not paying, you can excuse yourself to go to the ladies'
room when the bill comes. Don't think you need to prove to
him you can afford drinks or dinner. Don't feel you need to
pay, so you don't owe him anything. There is no *quid pro quo*
for a Rules Girl. You don't have to sleep with him because he
bought you a drink and a pricey appetizer!

Day 164: Holding Back

WEDNESDAY

If you get easily hurt, you can do *The Rules* by waiting for the other person to contact you first and acting less interested. A bisexual client had a fling with a man he met on Tinder and immediately felt the desire to be exclusive. He wanted to text him that he forgot his watch at his place as an excuse to see him again. We told him not to. Sure enough, the other man texted that he would mail the watch to him and said nothing about another date. While our client was upset, he realized he avoided a hookup or fantasy relationship by holding back.

Day 165: Keeping It Short

THURSDAY

Women are shocked when we tell them to end calls after ten minutes. They are used to talking for hours and feel it's rude getting off so quickly. Here's a tip: The best way to keep the conversation short is to not ask any questions or go into detail. If he asks, "How was your day?" say "Good." Don't reply, "How was your day?" back. Keep it short and sweet. If you don't ask anything, he will be forced to ask another question or two and then cut to the chase: "Can I see you this weekend?" Remember you can talk on the date. Become a good conversation-ender by saying, "I have a big day tomorrow," or "Sorry, that's my boss (or mother) on the other line."

Day 166: Boundaries

FRIDAY

Many women feel guilty about ending dates first, thinking that it's impolite. While men have no problem skipping
Valentine's Day, women feel rude about cutting things short.
Don't! Remind yourself that you have a life and other things
to do besides him. Tell yourself your time is valuable and you
need to go. If a man likes you, he will not be angry that you
ended the date first. He will ask you out again. Remember,
you're not being rude—you're practicing radical self-care.
Look at your watch after an hour or so and say, "Wow, this
was fun, but I have to go." Everyone wants a girl who is busy!

Day 167: Codependence Kills

SATURDAY

Another turnoff is being overly involved in a man's life. Some
women meet a man, and within a few weeks or months,
they try to patch up his relationship with his sister or best
friend. They try to help him get a job by introducing him
to their well-connected uncle. Or they introduce him to
their therapist for couples' counseling or put him in touch
with their nutritionist or trainer or decorator. He becomes
their pet project. This is called codependency, and it can kill
a relationship, as most men will feel smothered and rebel.
Rules Girls do nothing of the sort. They are busy with their
own lives!

Day 168: Intimacy
SUNDAY

We suggest not getting intimate on the first date, or second or third for that matter. But what if you've had a few drinks and you're really attracted to your date and one thing leads to another and it happens? Is all lost? Not necessarily! You can still practice *The Rules* by acting nonchalant and ending the date quickly, as opposed to lingering and acting needy and putting pressure on the guy to define the relationship now that you've slept together. It's not the physical act per se, but the clinginess afterward that often torpedoes a new relationship. But if you can't be intimate on the first date without being clingy, then don't be intimate on the first date!

Apply *The Rules* to Achieve Your Higher Self

1 If you can't drink without being intimate on a date, then don't drink. But if you are intimate, at least don't be clingy. End the date first!

2 If you left something inexpensive at your boyfriend's place, like your T-shirt or blow-dryer, don't use that as an excuse to text or call him. Let him notice it and contact you! Better to buy another shirt or blow-dryer than call him!

3 If you're a caretaker type, make sure you don't overfunction in your relationship. Resist the urge to do his errands or write his term paper, because you're not his assistant—you're his girlfriend and have errands and work of your own!

WEEK SEVEN
How's It Going?

Your *Rules* Weekly Pep Talk

It's been a couple of months . . . How are *The Rules* working for you? It takes practice, and it's easy to make lots of mistakes when you're dating because there are so many variables and different situations you can get yourself into. It is easy to justify, "I'll just do it this once," and then you fall into the tunnel of non-*Rules* and fly by the seat of your *Lower Self.*

Did you sleep with a new guy, thinking that's the best way to seduce him? Are you nagging your boyfriend, hoping to change him? Are you airing all your thoughts and dreams on social media? Did you just ask an online guy out for drinks? It's okay, tomorrow is a new day and you can start over using *The Rules* again.

This week, focus on looking back over the last three months you have been practicing *The Rules.* Which of your behaviors simply don't work, specifically premature intimacy, nagging, oversharing, and pursuing? Maybe review, recharge, and start dating again with a new perspective!

HOW'S IT GOING?

Daily *Rules*

Day 169: Twice a Week

MONDAY

In the second month of dating, you can see a guy twice a week if he asks. If he doesn't ask for more than Saturday night, then see him once a week. But typically a guy will want to see you three or four times a week in the beginning, and you will have to say no. You can say, "Sorry, crazy busy during the week." Keep it to the weekends or see him once during the week and on Saturday night. If you see a guy more than twice a week in the second month, he will not think you are that busy or special and could become bored and lose interest. Better to see him less and leave him wanting more!

Day 170: Don't Be Intimate So Fast

TUESDAY

Some women feel that the only way to get their date to commit is to sleep with him, hoping to create a special emotional connection. Choosing not to sleep with another person too soon is not about being mean, it's smart. There's a mind-body connection for a woman that doesn't exist as much in a man. A woman often gets emotionally attached after intimacy. Even an ardent feminist can feel devastated if a man doesn't call the next day. The other reason not to sleep with a date too fast is that you want him to fall in love with your soul first, not just your body. Your soul is your *Higher Self*, your character, what makes you unique. Don't sell yourself short by using your body to connect before your mind. Often these people suffer from low self-esteem and *Lower Self* feelings of unworthiness. In reality, sleeping with another person right away might make them not respect you or treat you like a lifelong partner.

Day 171: Dealing with Time-Wasters

WEDNESDAY

If you're single, every minute counts in your search for your soulmate. You have no time to waste with people who get in your way. News flash: Men are not the only time-wasters! Women—whether friends, coworkers, neighbors, or acquaintances—can eat up your time or chew off your ear on the phone or in person. How do you politely handle them? Say the same thing we tell you to tell men: "Sorry can't talk, work is crazy busy." But if they know you're not working because it's the weekend or you're retired, say you're doing house repairs or charity work. If it's on the phone, talk to them while you are on the treadmill, doing the laundry or paperwork, or going for a walk so you kill two birds with one stone. Sometimes you can put your phone on mute while they talk because there are people who can just talk or complain for an hour, and they won't even know that you've taken a shower while putting the phone on mute—you come back and they're still talking! Time is everything, so don't let anyone waste yours!

DAY 172: What Are We?

Slow down! Don't be the girl who says, "Now that we've slept together, what are we?" Don't be the one suggesting serious talks after intimacy or spooning or cuddling or cooking breakfast together and hanging out. Be the girl who jumps out of bed, brushes her hair, looks at her watch, and says she has to get going to work or the gym. The man has to bring up not dating other people and getting off dating apps. If it's not his idea to be exclusive, it will not work. If you bring up exclusivity, he might just agree to keep sleeping with you or to be polite, but his heart won't be in it. Say nothing!

Day 173: Don't Be Parental

People don't like to be told what to do. So if you don't want your significant other to dread seeing you, avoid your calls at work, or walk out of whatever room you're in, don't nag. Nagging reminds him of a parent, is annoying, and doesn't work, as he will ultimately do what he wants to do. Say what you want once and nicely and never again, and don't threaten or embarrass him in front of his family and friends about it. You can even try reverse psychology and pretend you agree with him about his destructive behavior. "That's great you are filing a tax extension and binge-watching TV instead!" Think about what you would be doing if you weren't nagging him...and do that!

Day 174: Don't Be Flattered

SATURDAY

Whether you're on Facebook, Instagram, or TikTok, it's easy to reveal too much about your personality and every move you make. Social media is about instant and effortless connections, while *The Rules* are about intrigue and mystery. Don't be flattered by a person viewing your story (trust us, they are viewing many stories,) or as we've said, even DMing you to meet up spontaneously because you're in the same area. They might say, "Oh, I see you're at Starbucks. Want to meet for coffee in an hour?" Don't jump up and down. There's nothing special about last-minute anything. It's nothing until they ask you out on a date several days in advance.

Day 175: Undoing Dating Mistakes

SUNDAY

If you just asked a guy out to dinner and then read this book, say, "Sorry, something came up." That is, if he even remembers. If he forgot, then you forgot. You can start *The Rules Handbook* now. If you baked him cookies, give them to your neighbor or a friend. If you invited him to your friend's wedding and he hasn't invited you to anything comparable, you don't have to go through with it. You can get out of it by saying, "Sorry, but my friend had to cut her guest list down, so I can't bring anyone." Don't be a slave to your past bad habits. You can undo whatever you did and become a Rules Girl now!

Apply *The Rules* to Achieve Your Higher Self

1 You can change your mind! Yes, you can! So if you just asked a guy out and are now reading this book, pretend you never asked. It never happened. If he remembers and confirms, just cancel. It's that simple!

2 If you are about to tell a guy "I prefer calls to texts" or "I need my birthday to be celebrated in a big way," stop! Don't tell him what to do; observe his behavior and then decide if he's right for you. Control is an illusion! He might oblige for a while, but he will eventually revert back to himself, a texter who does very little for your birthday.

3 If a guy texts you on the weekend and you don't have a scheduled date, ignore him. You're busy, unavailable, and not glued to your phone. If he wants to talk, let him take you out next weekend!

WEEK EIGHT
Buyer Beware Dating

Your *Rules* Weekly Pep Talk

Most people struggle with self-worth or where to draw
the line when someone does not treat them well or is
disrespectful. It's even harder to set boundaries when you
love someone and they speak unkindly to you or, even worse,
say cruel things to you. How much are you willing to take
before you say enough is enough, no matter how much
they love you?

Are you putting up with men who put you down?
Are you indulging online time-wasters who ask dozens of
questions but don't ask you out? Are you ignoring red flags
like anger and rudeness? Are you taking trips with men you
barely know instead of waiting for your honeymoon? If you
answered yes to any of these questions or similar ones, it's
time to reflect, reset, and possibly break up.

This week, focus on valuing your time, your standards,
and your long-term goals. Look back at your dating
character list and weed out the unhealthy people in your life
until you can meet the healthy ones who love and honor you.

BUYER BEWARE DATING
Daily *Rules*

Day 176: Buyer Beware Men
MONDAY

When a man likes you, he doesn't impose on you in any way or ask any questions that might annoy or embarrass you. So if an online guy asks you for more photos or keeps asking what other movies you like besides the three you already mentioned in your profile, ignore him and move on. He's a time-waster. He doesn't need more photos or to know every movie you like to ask you out. If a man complains that you don't text more often or are too quiet, it's not good. When a man likes you, he thinks you're perfect, or at least perfect for him. He is just happy to be texting the pretty girl!

Day 177: Crazy Questions
TUESDAY

People who ask, "Why are you on this app?" or "What are you looking for?" or "What's your idea of a perfect date?" or "Why are you still single?" or "Why did your last relationship not work out?" are interested in chatting, not dating, or they're married or just don't like you. Don't answer. It's obvious that you are on a dating app to meet people, and it's none of their business why you are still single. Don't get insulted and write back "I can't believe you're asking me such personal questions..." People who react at all waste time. Delete! You want dates, not crazy fights with strangers.

Day 178: A Week is Almost a Honeymoon

WEDNESDAY

A recent *Rule*-breaking trend is premature traveling. Couples who barely know each other are hopping on planes. Women get excited because they think the guy must like them if he wants to spend so much time together. No, he wants to sleep with you or have a plus-one for an event! So you can imagine their disappointment when we tell them they can't go away so soon. We explain that a week or even more away is a honeymoon and too much togetherness can make a guy go backwards. We tell them to say, "Sorry, but I can't get away." It's more important to get the guy than to see the Grand Canyon!

Day 179: Creepy

THURSDAY

Any new or online guy who asks you if you like to cuddle or brings up intimacy or favorite positions in a text or call is a *Buyer Beware*. If a guy asks you what you got from Santa or what your favorite color is, delete. You are not five-year-olds, and it's just too silly and creepy. If he says he noticed on your dating app that you like Italian food and wants to know what dishes, you can say pizza. But if he asks what topping, delete. If he wants to know your favorite topping, let him buy you dinner. Do not indulge these guys who ask one hundred questions. They get four messages to ask you out and that's it!

Day 180: Just Not into You!

FRIDAY

Realize quickly if he's just not into you. Some people are turned off when their date asks them to split the check because they don't think he's going to be a "good provider." But being a good provider is not the real issue. The actual issue is that if a guy is thinking about the bill, he's not thinking about you...your hair, your smile, your eyes, and how he's going to get you to agree to another date. It's a red flag—he's not that into you! When someone you're dating likes you, money is the last thing on his mind. Your future partner would never ask you to pay. He would think about the next interesting restaurant or movie he is going to take you to!

Day 181: Complainers

SATURDAY

A guy texted a woman after their first date that he had to get something off his chest. He said he felt "rushed" during their one-hour drinks and wondered if she was too busy for him. That text in and of itself was a red flag. A guy interested in dating you would simply ask for another date to spend more time with you, instead of complaining that you didn't give him enough time. When they like you, they rarely find anything wrong with you. But determined to salvage the situation, she reassured him she was not too busy to date him, that he just needed to ask her out again. He still didn't ask her out! Next!

Day 182: Window-Shoppers
SUNDAY

Ignore guys who ask for more photos or more anything! If he can't decide if he likes your looks based on your two or three online photos, then he's crazy or just window-shopping, not buying. Remember, you are a busy Rules Girl. You don't have time to send more photos! You also don't have time to write long-winded answers to questions. So if a guy asks how was your weekend, don't say, "Good, my cousin and I went shopping," just say "Really good!" If a guy complains about your two-word answers, then he's a complainer, not a dater. Longer conversations happen on the date!

Apply *The Rules* to Achieve Your Higher Self

1   Don't feel you have to answer every question an online guy asks! If he asks how your weekend was, what do you do for fun, when your last relationship was, and how long have you been on dating apps, answer one or two. Write back, "Good, I like to hike on weekends."

2   If he asks over drinks why you got divorced, don't say, "My ex is a jerk" or "He was cheating on me the whole time." TMI and unflattering for you! Just say, "We grew apart." More than that is none of his business!

3   Just because a guy asks you for a photo doesn't mean you have to send it. If he wants a photo, let him ask you out and take a photo or selfie on the date.

WEEK NINE
Sometimes You're Going to Get Hurt

Your *Rules* Weekly Pep Talk

Pain is inevitable, but suffering is optional! If you don't want to get overly hurt by the people you date in your life, invest the least into the relationship until they fully commit to you with proactive actions, heartfelt words like "I love you," and exclusivity, and talk about having a future together.

You will know based on their actions and words how much of your emotions, time, and energy to invest in them. Are they taking you out on consecutive Saturday night dates and giving gifts for your birthday and holidays? If they are not responding to *The Rules* positively and falling deeper and more madly in love with you, invest little to nothing.

This is not a game—it's self-preservation. Women who spend too much time, energy, or money—cooking dinners and offering "two tickets to a show"—into a new relationship are making a poor investment and will be devastated when it inevitably ends.

This week, soften the blow of any possible disappointments or a breakup by investing more in you and less in a guy that may never be in your future.

SOMETIMES YOU'RE GOING TO HURT
Daily *Rules*

Day 183: Just a First Date
MONDAY

If your date can't meet you at a public place, then don't go on the date. A gay client called us because a woman she met online rejected her. Their first date was seven hours because the woman didn't have a car, so she drove to her place to pick her up. Our client, being the more feminine one, texted the woman that she wanted to see her again, but the woman said, "I'm not feeling it." Our client was heartbroken. We said sorry and shared that we thought she invested too much into the date by driving to her place and that seven hours was too long. If your date can't borrow a car or take transportation to meet you, then you don't go! Rules Girls are not Uber drivers; they play it safe. We told her to treat women like men and let them pursue her so she doesn't get hurt again!

Day 184: Don't Judge
TUESDAY

If you feel that a person in your life is being cold or unavailable, don't assume the worst. They may not be a bad friend because she forgot your birthday on the actual day or didn't return your calls or texts right away. Don't attack and send them an angry double-text. Who knows what they are going through, and it may have nothing to do with you. It could be that they are overwhelmed: Her cat is sick or her car broke down, and your text got lost amongst the chaos in her life. Yes, we know it only takes a second to text back, but it's better to be compassionate (*Higher Self*) rather than cut them out of your life (*Lower Self*) because they're swept up in a tornado. When you choose to be empowered, you go with the flow and are understanding even when a friend says, "I'll get back to you tomorrow," and it takes them a few days or a week to return your call. It's not like she didn't show up for your wedding or drive you to the emergency room. Ask yourself if you have always been the perfect friend. Probably not! Often they have more going on than you know, so don't judge lest you be judged.

Day 185: Forgive Yourself

WEDNESDAY

If you're new to dating, you may not understand what you're doing. A newly divorced woman, who slept with a man on the first date and then was horrified she did, called us the next day about what to do. She said, "It just happened, he swept me off my feet. Now I just got a text saying, *That was fun!* What should I write him back?" We said your *Lower Self* slept with him. Forgive yourself, but now you have to ignore him until he asks you out for a second date and pretend the affair never happened. We said don't text back, as he is being overly casual. You can be your *Higher Self* at any time, starting now!

Day 186: Low-Effort Dates

THURSDAY

Readers who follow *The Rules* are nice, but not doormats! They don't put up with lazy or low-effort dates. Any person who says, "Let me know when you're free . . . " instead of asking you out on a date or says he's "Not looking for anything serious," or "Not a big planner, so can you pick the place," or gripes that "You seem too busy for me," is a waste of time! When a guy likes you, he suggests a date, makes all the plans, pays, and doesn't want to be casual. He doesn't complain that you didn't write back sooner or use more words or aren't showing more interest. He invests high effort, and that means courtship.

Day 187: Right Response

FRIDAY

If a guy says something crude at the end of a first date like "Why don't we go to bed tonight and get that part out of the way?" don't say, "Why don't you buy me jewelry now and get that part out of the way?" Now, that would be funny if you were a stand-up comic, but since you're a Rules Girl you need to be charming. Say, "Thanks for drinks, but I need to be somewhere..." Any man who mentions intimacy on the first date is a Buyer Beware. There is no reason to come across as a gold digger. That's *Lower Self* and beneath you. Your girlfriends might say "You go girl," but it's still wrong!

Day 188: No Perfect Proposals
SATURDAY

A client was sure that her boyfriend was going to propose on New Year's Eve, but he fell asleep before the ball dropped. She was irritated but emailed us instead. We said don't show it. He proposed the next morning. Had she started a fight, who knows how the weekend would have ended? Other clients expect petals on the bed or a photographer hiding in the bushes and get annoyed when it doesn't look like *The Bachelor*. We believe that how a guy wants to propose is not the point. The fact that he wants to marry you is more important than a message in a bottle or fireworks!

Day 189: For Hopeless Romantics
SUNDAY

If you can take it or leave it when a date doesn't call after you sleep with him or after a few dates, good for you! But if you get easily attached, you might need a set of dos and don'ts. Before reading *The Rules*, a woman met a man on an airplane. He said, "This food is awful. Let's go out to dinner." They had dinner, and she was smitten. He said he would call her the next day but didn't. She called his office many times to see why he didn't call. His secretary told her to stop calling. If you call men uncontrollably or are hopelessly romantic, you need *The Rules*.

Apply *The Rules* to Achieve Your Higher Self

1   If a man is crude or sarcastic, don't copy his lack of class and just end the date as soon as possible.

2   If you have a compulsion to call a man for any reason, treat it with deadly seriousness like lying or stealing or jaywalking and don't do it.

3   If you don't want to get hurt, spend more time on your family, friends, work, and hobbies than on the relationship.

WEEK TEN

You Made It Past Three Months!

Your *Rules* Weekly Pep Talk

Our world is fast and furious, and dating has become a haphazard maze of land mines, where if you step on the wrong one, it will explode! *The Rules* are not for people who want excitement and uncertainty and don't mind being blown up again and again by unpredictable dating. *The Rules* are for people who want happy, healthy, stable, and long-lasting relationships.

Rules People take it slow and steady and don't share their entire life story on the first date or indulge in marathon phone calls in the middle of the night. We gradually let the other person discover all the mysteries about us and savor getting to know each other.

By the third month, if all is going well, you can see the person two or three times a week and share a little bit more about your past, your family, and your feelings. There is no need to whine and complain, just share the facts. And no, you still don't get to ask them out or move into their home or turn your dates into therapy sessions. This week, focus on revealing a little more about yourself, but not everything!

YOU MADE IT PAST THREE MONTHS!
Daily *Rules*

Day 190: Dating Feels Like Dieting
MONDAY

Women typically tell us they did *The Rules* strictly for the first three months and were thrilled with the results but then got comfortable and fell off the wagon. Sound familiar? Dating is like dieting! After following a food plan for three months, you lose weight and then eat all the foods you gave up, and suddenly the pounds pile back on. When you fall off *The Rules* wagon, the guy becomes casual and starts talking about hanging out. Don't stop dieting until you get to goal weight. Don't stop doing *The Rules* until you're engaged or at least in a seriously committed relationship.

Day 191: Three Times a Week
TUESDAY

In the third month, you can see him up to three times a week. If he asks for more, say "Sorry, crazy busy with work," or "Um, I already have plans," or "Oh no, it's girls' night out." If you see him all the time, the relationship will get casual real fast and he might start asking for space, which is the last thing you want to hear. It's not unusual for guys to ask for more time together, but when you give it to them, they get scared and lose interest. Better to leave him wanting more than leave him bored. Besides, what incentive will he have to marry you if he can see you seven days a week?

Day 192: Do It Mostly

WEDNESDAY

After the first three months of dating, it is not the time to stop following the rules and see him seven days a week. It's the time to get busy with work, friends, and hobbies, so you disappear in between dates and keep him interested. But just because you can't stick to the three-times-a-week plan doesn't mean you have to move in or throw *The Rules* out the window. If you can't do *The Rules* 100%, do it mostly or as much as possible. For example, you can text back in ten minutes instead of an hour, but try not to initiate texts. You can see him four times a week on a holiday weekend, but not five. You need to still follow the spirit of *The Rules*, that less is more with men, and you can't go wrong.

Day 193: Deal-Breaker

THURSDAY

While we don't suggest talking about marriage or children in the early stages of dating, if he mentions that he's not sure if he wants kids and you definitely want one or two, what do you do? This is not something to be mysterious about. You need to tell him that having children is a deal-breaker for you and if he's not sure or the answer is no, then there's no point in seeing him anymore. When Catherine Zeta Jones met Michael Douglas, the actor had a son from a previous marriage, so she made it clear that she "Couldn't imagine life without children." He agreed, and they have two children of their own!

Day 194: Open Up Gradually

FRIDAY

In the third month, you can share a little more about yourself if he asks, but don't be an open book or overshare or start posting about the relationship on social media. Talking a lot and posting are dead giveaways of interest. Would you ever talk or post about a relationship with a guy you're not interested in? No! So act like you're not that interested. Everything in *The Rules* world is slow and steady. The rest of the world is fast and furious. Remember, you're not an influencer or celebrity trying to sell a product . . . you're a Rules Girl trying to get a guy to propose, so be cool and reserved.

Day 195: Not About the Dishes

SATURDAY

When the honeymoon phase is over, most fights are not about what started the fight (who left the dishes in the sink) but hurt feelings. You want accolades and approval, to be thanked for doing the dishes, and he wants respect and doesn't want to be told he does nothing. So be careful before you say something disparaging. Your *Lower Self* wants to hurt him for not giving you more credit, but your *Higher Self* knows that approval comes from the inside or from calling your girlfriends. So pause before you speak. Think about your motives. Don't focus on the minutiae. Your relationship is more important than housework or misunderstandings.

Day 196: Gift Negotiation

SUNDAY

When you are dating, you can never bring up Valentine's Day, your birthday, or the holidays. If he doesn't think of these occasions, buy you a gift, or take you out on his own, then he's not Mr. Right. But when you're married, you can drop hints about what you really want. If there's a project like cleaning out the garage that your husband is procrastinating on, you can ask him to make it your Valentine's Day or holiday gift for positive reinforcement. It works! Some husbands would be thrilled that they are getting off easy by throwing out stuff instead of buying you jewelry! But if you really want jewelry, you can show him a link to something in your budget. Remember that you already have the most important piece of jewelry . . . your engagement ring!

Apply *The Rules* to Achieve Your Higher Self

1   By the third month, you can introduce him to family and friends if he's already introduced you to his tribe. Let him take the lead.

2   Instead of thinking, "Now that we're at the three-month mark and exclusive, I can do whatever I want," think, "If it's not broken, don't fix it." In other words, keep doing what you did to get him in the first place—don't call or text first, don't ask him out, and don't try to change him!

3   If you have to remind someone you're dating that it's your birthday or Valentine's Day, it's a "Next!" But if you're married, you can say that you'd like this or that gift.

COURSE 4

Effective Commitment and Communication

10 WEEKS

If you're like most women, you love to talk and share your thoughts and feelings throughout the day with the people you love. That's fine for girlfriends or your therapist or life coach or hairdresser, but not with your romantic partners. You want to keep the romance and mystery and need to know when and what to share and when to be quiet. Studies have shown men in particular love a challenge, dislike therapy, and get easily bored by too much communication. You will have much more power to attract him with silence than oversharing.

In the early stages of dating, the first three dates, it's best to talk less than your date does. Let them be mesmerized by your eyes, your hair, your laughter, and your most attractive qualities. Let them ask you questions like you're a guest on his podcast or talk show. Answer their questions in a light and breezy way with the fewest words possible. They will delight, and you will be like a breath of fresh air. Up until now they have probably had so many dates who overshared and chewed their ear off.

Communication is important but can often be overrated. Take a step back and think before you share. We live in a transparent society. We post everything we do, say, and feel on Facebook, Twitter, and Instagram. That's fine for social media, but for a romantic relationship, there needs to be some silence and mystery. You need to let your significant other eat breakfast while reading the news on his iPad without interrupting. It's not pleasant to share every thought in your head, especially if it's negative or needy. Let them initiate the conversation about commitment.

After two or three months of dating, you can share a little more, but still don't tell him your entire life story. By the time he says "exclusivity," "I love you," and "the future," you can reveal a little more. By the time your partner proposes, he should know all about you, your parent's messy divorce at twenty, your flunking the bar exam the first time at twenty-five, and so on. Even after they know all about you, don't share the stories as if they are your therapist or best friend. You have a therapist and friends for emotional sharing and problem-solving.

If you've been dating one to two years depending on your ages, and they have said nothing about your future together, marriage, or children, it's time to communicate and let go: "I've enjoyed our time together, but I can't keep dating you without agreeing about a future together." If your partner doesn't talk about a future with you, lovingly break off the relationship. Don't scream, "I can't believe you still haven't proposed. Everyone is asking me what's going on, and I don't know what to say. It's so embarrassing. What's the problem? If you don't give me a ring by Christmas, I'm out of here!"

The key to effective communication is to use the fewest words as gracefully as possible, with the least amount of drama. Before you set your letting go boundary, pause and think about what you're going to say so it doesn't get overly emotional and messy. Go over a script with a *Rules*-y friend.

In the movie, *When Harry Met Sally,* Sally talked to Harry as a platonic friend every night for hours on the phone and on lengthy walks. But when she realized after they slept together that she wanted a commitment, she had to go radio silent. In the end, it was the silence, the unreturned phone calls, and the no-contact—not hundreds of silly chats—that made Harry finally propose. The most effective communication to get a commitment is selective and strategic communication.

WEEK ONE

Have You Committed Yet?

Your *Rules* Weekly Pep Talk

Consider how you are communicating in your committed relationship with your dating partners. Have you been following *The Rules*? Did you take your time getting to know them? Did you create romance and mystery during your courtship?

The Rules run counter to society. Society tells us to share everything with our partner, like a therapy session, to be transparent, to have no filter, to not suppress a single thought or feeling. We know this doesn't work because when we are in a committed romantic relationship, not everything we think or say needs to be shared, is useful, or is the truth.

Your partner is not supposed to fix you or complete you. They are meant to dance, play, and share your life with you. They are not to fill the roles of your parents, family, friends, therapists, coaches, coworkers, or bosses. And neither are you. You can't change anyone else, but you can shift the relationship dynamic by changing how you interact with others and by the choices you make.

This week, reflect on what role your romantic partner plays and is expected to play in your life. Are you parenting or bossing them around? Or vise versa? If either of you is playing any other role than that of a loving partner that delights in each other and has fun together, stop and reread *The Rules*.

Daily *Rules*

Day 197: Nothing's Changed
MONDAY

Young people like to say that dating is different today, that
there are no rules, that anything goes, that anyone can ask
anyone out, and that it's mutual. Not true! The only thing
that's changed is technology. There are new ways to make
contact on Facebook, Instagram, TikTok, dating apps,
and texting. Besides that, everything's the same. He has
to make the first move in person or online and lead your
couple's dance. He has to pick the place and time and make
reservations. And he has to pay. You only have to show up,
listen, be genuinely interested, and end the date first. The
dating dance has not changed because of technology.

Day 198: Not Your Friend
TUESDAY

In the early stages of dating before your date confesses, "I
love you," or asks, "Let's be exclusive!" or says, "I see a future
for us," your romantic partner is NOT your friend. We're
not trying to be negative here, just realistic. Remember, a
man has the power to stop calling or asking you out, to waste
your time, to say "I'm not sure how I feel about you," and
to break your heart. That's why investing too much time
and energy in the first two months will not serve you. We
don't recommend whirlwind courtships where couples are

inseparable. These fast-paced relationships fade out as fast as they get started. The person you are dating is not important in your life until he's your boyfriend or future husband.

Day 199: Why You Don't Say Anything First

WEDNESDAY

Even if you're in a committed relationship, don't say, "I love you" or "I miss you" first. He should lead in every dating step: the first to ask you out, the first to friend you, the first to follow you on social media, the first to text after your first date, the first to ask you out again, and the first to lead with physical affection. Don't initiate hugs, cuddling, kisses, or time together. Women in committed relationships sometimes feel entitled to suggest coming over, studying together, watching Netflix, or cooking together after only a few months of dating. If he's too tired or busy, you will feel rejected. *The Rules* are about staying in your power and not getting hurt. If a relationship is not working out, the woman most definitely should say first, "I want out." This is not pursuing, but self-care. However, if she asks to go to couples therapy, she runs the risk of him saying no. He has to want to go to therapy.

Day 200: Do the Math

THURSDAY

Always give less and do less with a man you are interested in. So if he writes ten words in a text, write back five. If he takes ten minutes to write back, take twenty minutes or even an hour, but switch it up so he doesn't think you're playing a game or are following a handbook. Use our "Text-Back Time Chart" from *Not Your Mother's Rules* as a guide to determine when to write back. Texting back in nanoseconds reeks of desperation and shows that you have nothing going on or have no self-control. Remember, you are busy with work and social plans, so don't drop everything to text!

Day 201: Don't Ask

FRIDAY

It is not a good idea to use holidays or events or milestones as an excuse to contact a guy. Don't text him, "Did you get your taxes done, or are you filing an extension?" Don't reach out to say, "Happy President's Day!" or "I remembered your parent's anniversary is coming up ;)" or "How did your review at work go? Are you getting that promotion?" or "I know your dad died five years ago today. Are you OK? I'm here if you need to talk." Don't text! He'll volunteer anything you need to know. He might figure out that you're using these holidays or occasions as a ploy to manipulate him or to remind him you exist.

Day 202: Fake Anniversary

SATURDAY

In the old days, couples celebrated their wedding anniversaries, meaning the day they walked down the aisle. Now some people want to celebrate all kinds of monthly first-date anniversaries. A woman told her boyfriend that the three-month anniversary of their first date was coming up. She bought him a card and a gift and expected the same. He thought dinner was enough. She got upset and showed him a necklace she liked. He bought it, but it was a hollow victory because a week later he broke up with her, citing, "I have crazy work hours and don't have time to date." She got the necklace, but she lost the guy.

Day 203: No Contact

SUNDAY

If your romantic partner has not talked about your future together or proposed, it's time to ask him where things are going. "I've enjoyed our time together and care about you, but I'm old-fashioned. I'm sorry, but I can't keep dating you without agreeing about our future together and having a formal commitment." If he says he is not sure or scared or doesn't talk about ring-shopping, ask him to contact you when he is ready. Many women give an ultimatum but don't do the no-contact part. They continue to accept calls and dates. This defeats the purpose of knowing your worth and setting him free. If he comes back with a ring, great—if not, next! Men often only propose when they realize they lost you after you're no longer sitting right next to them. It's a big step in a man's life, so don't take it personally if he needs a little time away.

Apply *The Rules* to Achieve Your Higher Self

1   With men, less is more when it comes to communication. They don't like being lectured or having lengthy conversations into the middle of the night. Say what you mean once in the fewest words possible and then see what happens!

2   Don't participate in a fake breakup. This is where the guy ends the relationship but still wants to be friends with benefits so you continue to talk and see each other with no future. That's like being fired and working for the company for free! We think not!

3   Don't make up reasons to celebrate your relationship, such as the anniversary of your first kiss, first date, or first trip. There's only one anniversary, and that's your wedding anniversary!

WEEK TWO

When In Doubt, Follow *The Rules*

Your *Rules* Weekly Pep Talk

When in doubt, follow *The Rules*! When a doctor gives you a prescription for cough medicine and advises you to "Take two teaspoons every four hours," you don't doubt his or her advice. You follow his directions. You don't take four teaspoons every two hours, and you don't drink the entire bottle at once. Ditto for dating.

We believe *The Rules* is a foolproof formula, so if you follow our advice, you will create healthy, loving, and long-lasting relationships with everyone in your life. If you apply this time-tested wisdom, you will avoid heartache, save time and money, and capture the heart of your lifelong partner. It's your choice not to follow *The Rules*, but you're flirting with disaster and will become disheartened.

This week, focus on following the Weekly Pep Talk and Daily Lessons. If you make a mistake, it's okay, try again. You can't change anyone else. You can only shift the relationship dance by changing how you interact with others and by the choices you make.

WHEN IN DOUBT, FOLLOW *THE RULES*
Daily *Rules*

Day 204: Anxiety Reliever
MONDAY

The Rules prevent you from being a nervous wreck or having to make emergency appointments with your therapist
or life coach or psychic. You're not sitting by your phone on
Friday or Saturday night biting your nails or pulling your
hair out, waiting to see if you have a date for the weekend.
If he doesn't ask by Wednesday for Saturday night, he either
doesn't like you enough or has been spoiled by non-*Rules* dat-
ers and needs to be silently inspired when you're not available
at the last minute. Either way, you make other plans or go out
with your girlfriends.

Day 205: Present an Obstacle
TUESDAY

If you want to make a man who spoke to you first fall head
over heels, just tell him he's not your type; he's too young or
old; that you only date men who are divorced, not separated;
that you're not over your ex; or give him literally any type
of obstacle. He will take it as a challenge and try to change
your mind and win you over. A divorced client with a child
was adamantly against dating her coworker, five years
younger and never married. He wouldn't stop asking her out,
and they're engaged now. He didn't want any other female
coworkers who were interested in him.

Day 206: A Little Pregnant

WEDNESDAY

Sometimes a woman will ask if she can break the first rule, *Don't Speak to Any Man First*, and then do all the other rules. She feels some men might need a little push and then she can convince him to want something more later on. We say unfortunately no, it's like being a little pregnant. It's like an alcoholic saying, "I'll just have one drink." The first rule is the most important rule. The beginning is everything unless it was a case of you beating him to the punch. It's better to do the first rule and break the others than to break the first rule and do the others. You can't undo the beginning. If a man doesn't start things, it's usually over!

Day 207: Deceptively Delicious

THURSDAY

Some women argue *The Rules* are deceptive because you're pretending you're not available or that you don't care as much as you do. But complete transparency can come across as crazy. You can't tell a guy, "I can't see you because you didn't ask me by Wednesday for Saturday night." Just like you wouldn't tell your kids, "I'm putting spinach in your brownies for your own good." You just say, "Sorry I'm busy," or "Enjoy your brownie." Comedian Jerry Seinfeld's wife, cookbook author Jessica Seinfeld, wrote *Deceptively Delicious* about sneaking nutrients into desserts. It's not lying—it's just not volunteering information.

Day 208: Short and Sweet
FRIDAY

Women are always asking us how to get off the phone in ten minutes or how to keep messaging on dating apps to a minimum. The key is to not ask any questions, so there's nothing to talk about but the next date. If you ask the same questions back every time he asks, "How are you? How was your weekend?" the conversation will go on forever. Pretend you're a movie star being interviewed on TV and ask nothing back. If you just say "Good," he will figure out that the only way to get you to talk is to set a date. Better to seem a little cold or rude than to get stuck on the phone for an hour!

Day 209: Don't Remind Him
SATURDAY

Men in love are not cynical about Valentine's Day. They don't say, "This is just a commercial holiday!" or "Valentine's Day flowers are a rip-off." Any man who talks like that will probably also say, "Marriage is just a piece of paper." Cynicism and love do not mix. However, some men like to be more creative than romantic about gifts. Women anxiously wait to see if the guy they are dating is going to do anything. Will he remember or skip it? Will he be practical or romantic? Ideally, he will ask you out a week or two in advance for dinner. Ideally, you will receive a card that says love and something romantic like candy, flowers, or jewelry. Don't drop hints about the holiday. If you have to remind him, then it doesn't count. *The Rules* are like truth serum. You watch his behavior and know where you stand.

Day 210: Wonderful Payoff

SUNDAY

The Rules might seem retro and politically incorrect, but they work. Being a career woman, you might find it hard to be feminine when you're home, but force yourself. Switch your mindset from conquering the world to being kind to the man who married you. Reset your focus from finance to romance. There's no point in being a success at work and a failure at home. Family comes before work. When you're being your *Higher Self*, he won't take the long way home or tell his friends that you're a ball and chain or that marriage is a lot of work—he'll brag that you're the best wife, he'll remember and celebrate your birthdays and anniversaries, he'll buy you flowers for no occasion, he'll want to spend more time with you, and he'll never want to get divorced.

Apply *The Rules* to Achieve Your Higher Self

1 If you met the man of your dreams and he's a real catch, don't make it so easy for him like every other girl. Think of something you don't like about him and think about that, "I don't know, he might be too short for me!" He will sense that you are not that interested and work harder to win you over.

2 We get it, you're a badass career woman, but when you come home, don't act like a CEO but a CUAO and switch from masculine to feminine energy.

3 *The Rules* for marriage are the opposite of *The Rules* for dating. As much as you were hard to get is as much as you need to be easy to be with! You can be a badass at work, but be a good egg at home.

WEEK THREE
Watch for Red Flags

Your *Rules* Weekly Pep Talk

When you follow *The Rules*, you will become more discerning and look out for relationship red flags that will save you from dating Buyer Beware dates. We have heard so many tragic dating stories from our clients that truly made our hearts ache for them. All the signs were there at the very beginning, yet women often project onto their dates what they want them to be versus seeing clearly who they are and what their actions or non-actions are saying.

If your date cancels on you for a trivial reason, cancels more than once, skips a week, or is secretive about his phone, don't get mad or get even. Ignore him. Next! Don't create an imaginary vision of him and then become blindsided by his bad behavior.

This week, think about and look for red flags in every interaction and on every date. Keep your antenna up so you can see and hear clearly if he is not-husband material.

Daily *Rules*

Day 211: No Revenge
MONDAY

Hell hath no fury like a woman scorned! If you find text
exchanges between your boyfriend and another woman,
there's nothing wrong with calmly confronting him and
getting to the bottom of it. Sometimes a clingy ex will
contact your man and there's nothing he did wrong. But if
he is flirting or behaving badly, break up with him. Don't
do what some women do: send screenshots to his family to
embarrass him or post screenshots on social media to ruin
his life. When you air your dirty laundry, it's obvious you
have nothing going on. Your *Higher Self* says breaking up and
moving on is the best move.

Day 212: It's a Sign
TUESDAY

Canceling a date is the kiss of death. When a man really
likes you, he would never think of not seeing you unless it's a
genuine emergency, like if he was in a car accident (even then
he could figure out a way to Uber over) or his mother had
a stroke. Canceling on you would be like missing fifty-yard
line seats at the Super Bowl, so it would never be for a flimsy
reason. When a man cancels because he's working late or
tired or has a lot going on, he's just not that into you. When
a man likes you, you're his priority. Not FaceTime or Zoom,

but in-person dates. If he cancels more than once without an emergency reason . . . It's a next!

Day 213: Pull Back

WEDNESDAY

We don't believe in confronting people, because you rarely get the reaction you want and might come across as needy. Pulling back works better. In the series *And Just Like That* (the *Sex and the City* reboot), Carrie asks Miranda if she's going to answer the phone when her nonbinary lover Che calls. Miranda responds, "I want to, but I'm not. I've been too available." Carrie says, "So you're doing *The Rules* now? You're going to tell them you can't go out tomorrow night because you're washing your hair?" Miranda ignores Carrie's sarcasm and thinks pulling back is the most effective option so she doesn't get hurt again.

Day 214: Don't Force Him to Talk

THURSDAY

Most men are like cavemen—wired to win—so if you're fighting, expect to lose because a man will figure a way to succeed, whether it's by telling you he doesn't want to talk right now, watching sports, putting on headphones, or even leaving the house. Don't force him to talk when he's not in the mood, especially in the middle of the night. Women find talking therapeutic and want to get out every feeling to solve the problem—men not so much. So wait until he's ready to talk and then revisit the issue. Scheduling the talk when he's in a good mood, like on his day off or after the gym, can only help. Be considerate. Don't talk to him when he's watching a game or at work. He'll appreciate that you are not insistent or obnoxious. In marriage, sometimes losing is winning.

Day 215: Stop Wondering

FRIDAY

We created *one call or text* for closure, to eliminate unnecessary wondering about getting back an ex. Some women don't want to know the truth about their relationship. After a breakup, a woman emailed us to ask if there was any hope of getting back her ex from a year ago. We went over her situation and suggested she text him, "Hope you are OK, sorry I wasn't nicer." He wrote back, "Please don't contact me again." She was devastated, but we told her that at least now she can stop thinking about him and move on. Some women never get closure and spend the rest of their lives waiting, wondering, and not dating anyone else.

Day 216: Not Mutual

SATURDAY

It's trendy to say that love should be *mutual*. But we've noticed that the women who say that do not get devastated when a relationship doesn't work out. These women may have more masculine energy: They like skydiving and are not women who can't get out of bed and miss work when a guy doesn't call. Mutuality is good for BFFs, siblings, and coworkers, but not for men. Love works best when a man wants you more or you pretend you don't care as much as you do. Don't think a man needs encouragement, reciprocity, or mutual respect. He's a man—he doesn't.

Day 217: Drop Friends

SUNDAY

Not every friend or family member is going to be supportive of your *Rules* marriage. Some might think that you "could have done better" or "your husband is too bossy." They might say, "I wouldn't put up with that!" or "Why do you have to run everything by him?" If your friend is annoyed that you have to get off the phone when your husband comes home, encourages you to spend money when you're on a tight budget, or doesn't show respect for your marriage, you might want to distance yourself or even drop her. You can get another friend, but you can't always get another husband!

Apply *The Rules* to Achieve Your Higher Self

1   If you're making excuses for guys who cancel Saturday night dates because their college roommate is in town, then you're going to play second fiddle for the rest of your life. The only reason a guy should cancel is a car crash or because a relative is in the hospital.

2   If you're obsessed with an ex that you broke rules with, shoot your one shot with a quick call or text saying you're sorry and see if he bites. If he doesn't ask to meet, it's over and move on, but at least you know where you stand!

3   When you feel the tables turning against you in a relationship, don't force the other person to talk or pay attention to you. Just the opposite, pull back and see what happens. Don't force anything.

WEEK FOUR
Keep the Faith

Your *Rules* Weekly Pep Talk

How are you doing? Keep the faith that no matter how many "next" dates you have gone through, you'll eventually find your lifelong partner. We understand you may be tired of dating apps and meetups. Maybe you feel like giving up? Before you do, ask us or a certified *Rules* dating coach to look at your profile and photos and help you answer all your messages.

Getting a second opinion from an expert is important. Invariably, we have found that women who weren't meeting high-caliber men were either presenting themselves in an unflattering way or acting too eager. When we changed their profiles from dark and heavy to light and breezy and made their photos cooler and more contemporary, they immediately got results. When we helped them write back messages that were friendly but succinct, they got dates.

This week, focus on not quitting—get advice from someone who has studied or is a coach in *The Rules*.

KEEP THE FAITH
Daily *Rules*

Day 218: Try Again!
MONDAY

Some women feel they tried dating apps, but they didn't work. When we look at their profiles, we notice that they had written essays rather than two-sentence bios and that the photos were not flattering. Some women wrote they were cheated on in the past and looking for someone honest and trustworthy. TMI! Some women said that any man who messaged them would get "home-cooked meals and a dog walker." Calling all caretakers! We rewrote their bios and picked out prettier photos. When they revised their profiles *The Rules* way, they got results.

Day 219: Exceptions
TUESDAY

Are there any exceptions to *The Rules*? Rarely. A grade school teacher warmly greeted all the parents at a Christmas party. One parent was a widower who asked for her number, and now they are married. Did she speak to him first? Technically yes, but as part of her job, not in a romantic way. Before reading *The Rules*, another woman messaged a guy first on a dating app, but he said she beat him to the punch as he was going to contact her. She got lucky because he already thought she was cute. They are married now.

Day 220: Ultimatum

WEDNESDAY

Some women balk at the idea of giving a man an ultimatum. "Isn't that aggressive? I thought *The Rules* are not about forcing anything." Yes, *The Rules* are about being reserved, but after a year or two you would be a fool not to ask about the future if he hasn't brought it up. Most guys will date you for five years without a formal commitment if you let them, citing financial reasons, the divorce rate, their parent's divorce, global warming, yada yada! But a Rules Girl has a goal to get married.

Day 221: Believe Him

THURSDAY

You know the adage, "Don't listen to what a man says. See what he does." We believe you should listen to what he says *and* see what he does. So if he says "I don't have time for a relationship" or "I'm not looking for anything serious," believe him! Don't try to sell him on you or change his mind or give him more time. A man knows how he feels right away. If he doesn't feel a spark, it's over. A man can grow on a woman, and she can grow to like his personality if she's not initially attracted to him. But the reverse isn't true. A man can't grow to like a woman. He has to like her looks and personality type immediately.

Day 222: Don't Over-Thank
FRIDAY

You can't get a guy to like you by thanking him. Some
women will text, "Thanks for spoiling me with brunch."
Excuse us, but paying for brunch is not spoiling you. Don't
act like it's a big deal. A woman attending a seminar thanked
the speaker, hoping he would ask her out. He said, "You're
welcome." She called us asking if there was any chance
this could become romantic. We said no because he knows
what you look like and didn't suggest coffee or drinks. You
can't get a man to like you by thanking him! Besides, you
spoke to him first. If he were interested, he would have
approached you!

Day 223: Fake Closure
SATURDAY

If you don't hear from a guy after a few dates, don't use
that as an excuse to ask for closure. Closure is after a serious breakup. Don't remind him you exist or pin him down.
Don't follow up with, "I haven't heard from you...is everything OK?" Don't ask for clarity. Don't say, "I thought we
had something special." Closure is for women in a committed relationship who have been broken up with or ghosted
and want some explanation. Fake closure is when you're not
exclusive and want to know why he's not calling. He never
said "I love you" or "exclusive," so he doesn't owe you anything, not even a call. He's not interested. That's why he's not

calling, and he doesn't want the awkwardness of explaining that to you. Move on!

Day 224: Dead Zone

SUNDAY

Weekends and national holidays are the Dead Zone. That means you should not respond to messages or texts from men you don't have plans with from Friday at 6 pm to Monday at 10 am, or Tuesday at 10 am if Monday is a holiday. The reason you disappear and don't respond is because a Rules Girl has or creates plans. You are on a plane or on the beach or skiing or at tennis camp. You are not sitting at home in sweatpants, staring at your phone. If you answer texts during the Dead Zone, guys will think that you have nothing going on or are not that special. Guys are wired to want the girl who has a strong self-worth and is busy on weekends!

Apply *The Rules* to Achieve Your Higher Self

1 Don't think of the Dead Zone, ultimatums, and other rules as restrictions, but as rewards. Boundaries save you from being too available and your own worst enemy.

2 When a guy pays for drinks and dinner, immediately say "Thank you" and that's it. You don't need to send a *Thank you* text the next day. You thank him once in person and never think about it again.

3 If a date ghosts you, don't track him down and demand to know why. Maybe he didn't feel a connection, or he's not interested in a serious relationship, or he's back with his ex. He's not interested in you, and that's all you need to know.

WEEK FIVE
Disagreements and Fighting

Your *Rules* Weekly Pep Talk

We understand when people get angry or hurt, their emotions often explode out of control. It's hard to be calm when you are upset and feel you want to attack the person back who hurt you. Resist the urge to lash out or yell at the person, and just don't do it.

Fighting can bring out the worst in couples, and their *Lower Selves* take over. Pettiness, sarcasm, contempt, criticism, stone-walling, and one-line zingers intended to inflict pain on their partner do a lot of damage. As the saying goes, you always hurt the one you love.

Avoid fighting at all costs, or at least pick your battles so you don't become sensitive and end up arguing about everything. The *Lower Self* will often choose to yell or say nothing, as in silent scorn. The *Higher Self* actively listens, acknowledges their partner's feelings, knows it's okay to disagree, and suggests they discuss it later, when tempers have calmed down. There is almost always a way to communicate a different opinion without fighting. The best way to avoid fighting is to maturely acknowledge that "I hear you, and I'm sorry you feel that way," or "I'll take that in and get back to you," or "You may have a point. I'll think about it." Give yourself twenty-four hours to calm down before reacting or responding.

This week, focus on creating peace and harmony in your relationships, not minor battles that will lead to a great war. Is it more important to be "right" or "reconnected"?

DISAGREEMENTS AND FIGHTING
Daily *Rules*

Day 225: Hold Your Tongue
MONDAY

Did you ever have a fight that started with "I can't believe you made me late to my cousin's wedding!" and blew up into "You're always late!" Before you know it, you're mentioning everything he's done late in the last year, from buying your birthday present late to paying the credit card bill late and incurring a late fee. Your *Lower Self* is on a roll! Before you say more, remember that you used to go to weddings alone. You were the girl trying to catch the bouquet. Switch to your *Higher Self* and be more compassionate: "No one is perfect" and "Weddings rarely start on time anyway." And then thank him for driving!

Day 226: Don't Blow Up
TUESDAY

You want to blow up because you're trying to pay the mortgage down and spend carefully. Meanwhile, your husband just bought a new set of golf clubs. Or, you're the spender and your husband watches every penny. First, blow off steam by telling a friend, so by the time you talk to your husband, you're whispering and not screaming. Second, don't tell him golf is stupid. Don't keep score or be a bean counter. Your *Lower Self* wants to whine that life isn't fair and you're not compatible, but most couples think differently about finances. Hello *Higher Self* . . . remember you married him for love, and don't make everything about money.

Day 227: Don't Be Sarcastic
WEDNESDAY

A client shared with us that when she and her attorney husband would argue, rather than seeing his perspective, she would sarcastically say, "Oh, that's the lawyer in you arguing his case." It was her way of putting him down and deflecting the issue. Be careful to avoid passive-aggressive behavior. Her contempt made him even angrier. "This has nothing to do with my being a lawyer..." We told her that her comments were disrespectful. Your *Higher Self* is happy to listen, consider his point of view, and help to repair the misunderstanding as quickly as possible. *Lower Self* wants to be right and rub it in. If you don't agree with his point of view, just say "Sorry you feel that way," and say nothing mean.

Day 228: Silence is Golden
THURSDAY

Some women feel we are telling them to silence their voices by not arguing. What we are saying is that if you are going to say something unkind or sarcastic in return, you're going to escalate the situation instead of resolving it. You can say "Sorry you feel that way," but not "Look who's talking!" Before you blurt something out, pause and ask yourself if it's kind, necessary, or productive. Speak effectively because it's not about who is right or wrong, but what is most effective for a happy marriage.

Day 229: Respect
FRIDAY

Many couples argue over room temperature (he's hot, you're always cold), travel plans (he wants to go and do, you want to relax), money (he's frugal, you're a spender), or what time to eat (he's hungry at 5 pm, you're not). Jerry Seinfeld joked that going on vacation "is paying a lot of money to go fight in a hotel." It's tempting to speak from your *Lower Self* in a disagreement and say, "You're driving me crazy, leave me alone!" But if you say it enough, he might really leave. We all want respect, so summon your *Higher Self* to respond "I am going to let go and take the high ground because it's more important to be connected while we're on vacation," or "I guess we can agree to disagree." If you're cold, wear a sweater!

Day 230: Fight Prevention
SATURDAY

In a certain twelve-step program, you call someone so you don't pick up the first drink. It's easier to stay sober than to get sober. It's also easier to not say the first mean word than fight and make up. Don't wait until after you've said twenty mean things to contact us to stop you. You will save so much time and energy when you play the fight out and avoid it. A client told us she was hurt that her husband noticed she put on weight. She wanted to say, "You never notice anything good!" Instead, she called us, and we asked her if she put on weight. She replied yes. So, we said you're probably more upset with yourself. She agreed and dropped it.

Day 231: Compassion is the Best Response
SUNDAY

When your husband says something triggering or hurtful, don't try to get even. Summon all your strength not to take the bait, not to get even, and to be your *Higher Self*, even if he is being his *Lower Self*. For example, you have lower back pain and your husband smugly asks, "Can you pinpoint what you did or why it happened?" You tell him you think it was because you wore four-inch heels to his friend's wedding, and he pragmatically says, with no shred of sympathy, "Well, that doesn't sound possible." If you feel that's not the reaction you wanted, don't retaliate the next time he's not feeling well. Don't sarcastically say, "Can you pinpoint what you did or why it happened?" Just say, "Sorry you're not feeling well."

Apply *The Rules* to Achieve Your Higher Self

1   Treat the first mean word like the first drink for an alcoholic and don't say it. If you don't say the first mean word, you can't say the tenth.

2   When your husband is critical, ask yourself if there's any truth to what he is saying. If so, take correction instead of getting defensive or offended.

3   In a disagreement, instead of saying "You're always late. It's so annoying," say "I love it when you're on time." Reframing your words can make the difference between a fight and healthy communication.

WEEK SIX

Don't Give Up Yet on Committed Relationships

Your *Rules* Weekly Pep Talk

We understand that dating can be frustrating. You go on so many first dates and one guy is worse than the other! Don't give up yet! The thought of taking a break for a month or a year or giving up altogether is tempting. Or, maybe you've made up your mind that your life is going to revolve around your family, friends, work, and pets . . . Who needs a man? But if you're reading this book, there's still a part of you that longs for a life partner, someone to hold hands with at the movies, dance with at weddings, and grow old with in the nursing home.

Keep reading and dig deep inside your *Higher Self* to ignite the courage and persistence you need before you delete your dating apps and skip this week's speed-dating events. Don't fall into the hopeless thinking of your *Lower Self* and do anything rash.

This week ask yourself, "Who doesn't have three hours a week to look for a soulmate?" Schedule and make the time to get back in the dating arena and do your best!

DON'T GIVE UP YET ON COMMITTED RELATIONSHIPS
Daily *Rules*

Day 232: Never Give Up
MONDAY

A client called to say she was "giving up" on dating. The man she had high hopes for skipped Valentine's Day, and she was heartbroken. We asked, "What do you mean by giving up? Would you give up on breathing or looking for a new job or apartment if you were fired or had nowhere to live? Obviously not. Well, that's how you have to think about dating. There's always another man, another dating app, another singles event, another party." Rules Girls just don't give up—we wipe away a tear and move forward. Just when you're ready to give up, you can meet the person you will spend the rest of your life with. A woman's Buyer Beware boyfriend of five years broke up with her on New Year's Eve. She sat in her office crying as her boss walked in and asked her what happened. When she told him, he invited her to his family's New Year's Eve party. She was not in the mood for a party, as her mascara was running down her face, but fixed her makeup and forced herself to go for an hour. There she met her boss' younger brother, who is now her husband. You never know!

Day 233: Reaping Results

TUESDAY

No person would bother to do *The Rules* if they didn't get results. Being hard to get by not calling or suggesting plans, not being an open book, waiting to be intimate, and not going on trips requires self-control. So if there was no payoff, there would be no point! People who follow *The Rules* are realists. They're not naïve or living in a dream world, and they're willing to do what it takes. The payoff is having a healthy relationship and feeling secure because he pursued you and worked hard to get you. Rarely have we seen a *Rules* follower not get the love of her life!

Day 234: No Breaks

WEDNESDAY

You're dating and going to meetups, but you're still "not meeting anyone good." You want to take a break from going out and cancel all subscriptions. We ask, "Take a break from what? Meeting your life partner or future husband?" No, no breaks! You can take a break from looking at your online messages over the weekend during the Dead Zone, but don't take down your profiles. Many women actually met their future husbands right before they were going to give up. Persistence pays off. Don't give up!

Day 235: Misconception

THURSDAY

A common misconception is that you will meet someone when you're not looking or thinking about it. True, some women meet Mr. Right when they're busy running a marathon or visiting a friend at the hospital or returning a library book or walking their dog. But you can't count on chance encounters. You need to put yourself out there. We know that singles events like hiking, tennis, or skiing can feel awkward like summer camp, but what's the alternative? An Ivy Leaguer scoffed that singles events were beneath her, an insult to her intelligence, and never went. She's fifty-five years old and still single!

Day 236: Thinking versus Doing

FRIDAY

It's normal to think after a bad date or breakup, "That's it, I'm officially done with men!" But, thinking or feeling hopeless about finding love does not mean you have to act on it. Even if your heart isn't in it, you can still put makeup and a cool outfit on and go to a club for an hour. Even if you detest dating apps, you can still update your profile and post a few photos as an act of faith. If all the great authors and entrepreneurs quit when their books weren't published or their ideas were dismissed, we wouldn't have some of the best books and inventions we have today. Like it or not, it's the same for dating. Keep going!

Day 237: Look in the Mirror
SATURDAY

A thirty-nine-year-old client was at her wit's end. She was
ready to give up on getting married and having children. She
had tried everything to no avail: dating apps, singles events,
matchmakers, hiking (even though she hated to hike), golf
(even though she found it boring), and mixers at churches and
temples (even though she wasn't religious) to meet men. She
asked us, "Is there anything else I can do?" We asked her
to send us photos and noticed that her hair was excessively
short and her clothes were frumpy. We suggested a makeover
(longer hair and trendier clothes), and three months later, she
met her husband. Look in the mirror. Sometimes the answer
is that simple!

Day 238: Better Fit
SUNDAY

After a breakup, you might feel that there is no one as handsome or perfect as your ex (even though he broke your heart),
that he is your one and only, and every guy pales in compari-
son. Realize that's a ridiculous thought. There are eight bil-
lion people on the planet. How can he be the only one? Just
the opposite, clients who met their new boyfriend or husband
told us he was actually a better fit than their ex. While their
ex may have been more charismatic or this or that, they had
more in common with the new guy.

Apply *The Rules* to Achieve Your Higher Self

1   Instead of calling your ex, call every family member, friend, acquaintance, neighbor, and coworker to introduce you to new guys.

2   Instead of thinking, "Someday I'll go back to dating," do one thing today to meet a guy. There is no someday—there's only now.

3   Instead of thinking you blew it with your ex and your love life is over, think abundance. Play "It's Raining Men" by the Weather Girls, and believe that, as the song says, "each and every woman could find her perfect guy."

WEEK SEVEN

Time to Consider Moving On

Your *Rules* Weekly Pep Talk

Rules Girls never give up on love, but we do move on from romantic partners who don't choose or want to commit after a year or two or more of dating (depending on your age) or want to keep dating us while they figure it out. Most of our readers and clients want a loving and long-lasting relationship, followed by marriage and children. Investing your time, energy, and love into a relationship with someone who does not have the same long-term goals as you do is a bad investment.

After a year of committed dating, your partner should know if they want to spend the rest of their life with you. There is no reason to invest full-time energy in a relationship that will continue to be part-time with no future.

This week, focus on moving on (or moving out, if you are living together) if the person you have been dating long term has not proposed to you. There is no reason to see him or speak to him any longer if he doesn't know or can't decide if you're The One. After time passes, he can always call you when he has a ring and then you can accept it, assuming you're still available!

TIME TO CONSIDER MOVING ON
Daily *Rules*

Day 239: Commitment
MONDAY

If a guy doesn't talk about marrying you after a year or more of dating, then he's either seeing other women or doesn't see a future. You need to summon the courage to say to him, "I've enjoyed our time together, but I'm old-fashioned and don't believe in dating forever, so I was wondering where this is going." If he says that he's happy with the status quo, then say that's not going to work for you. If he says he sees a future but doesn't know when, then tell him to contact you when he does know. Don't date him while he figures it all out. Rules Girls don't waste time or date forever!

Day 240: Letting Go
TUESDAY

A woman wanted to break up with a Buyer Beware guy whom she suspected was cheating. She couldn't summon the courage to call it quits but accused him of womanizing so many times that he finally broke up with her. We said that she got the breakup she wanted, but she didn't see it that way. Rather than being happy and empowered by *Higher Self,* she was angry that he ended it first and wanted him back. She continued following him on social media to see if he was dating and made her life miserable, giving in to her *Lower Self.*

We told her to block him on social media, stop stalking him, and move on! She did and is happily dating someone else!

Day 241: Moving On
WEDNESDAY

After two years, a Rules Girl finally gave her boyfriend the "Where is this going?" speech. They were practically living together, but she was afraid to ask. He said he wasn't sure how he felt about marriage, but if she wanted a ring soon, he wasn't the guy. She called us in tears, wondering what to do. We said at thirty-three years old, post your profile on dating apps, go to social events, and tell everyone you know that you're newly single. She called all her girlfriends that night and asked them if they knew anyone. A week later, her friend set her up with her older brother, and a year later, they were married.

Day 242: No Negativity
THURSDAY

The point of support groups is to give support. If you have friends or are part of a forum on Facebook or elsewhere where women talk about how depressing dating is or how difficult it is to meet a nice guy, then you're in the wrong group. You want to be around women who talk about what actions they are taking (upscale bars, hikes, speed-dating events) and keep you accountable (tell someone your activities), not anyone who is making excuses (bad hair day or need a break from dating) or who is negative or sarcastic. You can be negative or sarcastic all by yourself!

Day 243: New Terms, Same Story

FRIDAY

There's a new vocabulary to explain men's bad behavior in the digital age. "Ghosting" is when a guy suddenly stops contacting you without any explanation. "Haunting" and "orbiting" means ghosting you but appearing on social media, such as liking your Instagram photo. "Breadcrumbing" means he is keeping you engaged with texts and calls and social media attention, but it goes nowhere. Whatever you call his behavior, the bottom line is he's not interested. A Rules Girl doesn't care about terminology, just dates. There's nothing new under the sun. If a guy isn't asking you out, online or off, there is nothing you can do. Women often ask us, "A guy at work (or church or the gym) is really cute, so how can I get him to ask me out?" Friends, family, and other dating coaches might say, "Stop by his desk, flirt, ask to borrow a pen, or invite him to lunch." We say, "Nonsense, don't waste your time. Don't talk to five girlfriends about him. He's not interested. There's nothing you can do. It's a fantasy." No need to be confused about dating or force a relationship out of desperation by your *Lower Self* by listening to bad advice. *The Rules* are truth serum and empower your *Higher Self*.

Day 244: Non-Breakup

SATURDAY

Many women contact us to say a guy broke up with them, yet they continue to call him and see him as if nothing happened. One guy broke up with his girlfriend of three years the week before Christmas, citing compatibility issues, but she had bought tickets to a New Year's Eve party and still wanted to go. She asked if he still wanted to, and he said, "Sure." We asked, "How is this a breakup if you're going to the party together?" Just because he said, "Sure" doesn't mean you're getting back together. Maybe he doesn't have better plans. If you want to get him back, let him miss you. Go to the party with a girlfriend or anyone but him! It's not a breakup if it's business as usual. A breakup means you don't see him so he misses you. No contact means no contact!

Day 245: Getting Him Back

SUNDAY

After a breakup, many women tell themselves that the best way to get back their ex is to see him a lot. They think, "Out of sight, out of mind." They also want to prevent him from meeting anyone else, as if that's even possible! So they stop over in a sexy outfit to cook him dinner or do his laundry, or they might get him two tickets to his favorite Broadway show or sports team. They might send his mother a holiday gift to show that they are not bitter and would make a lovely daughter-in-law. Some guys will not object to sex, free dinners, tickets to a show, or your being nice to their mother.

But don't be fooled, none of this will make a guy come back. If he's going to come back at all, it's when you disappear and date others. Absence, not availability, makes the heart grow fonder!

Apply *The Rules* to Achieve Your Higher Self

1 When a guy wants to break up, don't try to talk him out of it or be all over him to get him to change his mind. Say "No worries" and disappear. Next! Love only those who love you!

2 Don't call your ex's mother or sister or best friend to put in a good word for you. It reeks of desperation. Besides, no one can make your ex marry you!

3 Don't listen to anyone who says that the best way to get a guy's attention is to stop by his desk or run into him at the watercooler. These tactics don't work. He either notices you or he doesn't. Besides, you have better things to do than manipulate a meetup!

WEEK EIGHT
Breaking Up Is Hard to Do

Your *Rules* Weekly Pep Talk

Sometimes, unfortunately, relationships and marriages don't work out. There could be many reasons and circumstances as to the whys and wherefores, but what is most important is how you break up or consider if you should get back together.

Many clients contact us to get an ex back. No matter how slim the chances are, we go over every detail and pray for a miracle. They might ask, "What are the odds of getting him back? Fifty percent? Twenty percent? Tell me the truth. I can take it." You would think they were talking about a cure for cancer, such is the devastation of a breakup. Or they might say, "I can't talk to my mother about this. She won't understand. So tell me what you would tell your daughter if she were me?" Of course, we always tell the truth.

This week, focus on reality, not fantasy. As Saint Augustine said, "Work as though everything depended on you. Pray as though everything depended on God."

BREAKING UP IS HARD TO DO
Daily *Rules*

Day 246: No Interest
MONDAY

If someone breaks up with you, falls out of love, or changes
his mind about marrying you or staying married to you, he
has no interest. Maybe he once loved you but now he doesn't,
so it doesn't really matter how he used to feel. A person either
loves you or has no interest. If he doesn't want to be with you,
talk to you, or hear from you, he has no interest. We know
it sounds harsh, but in order for you to stop thinking about
him, we have to tell you the bitter truth. So please don't take
it the wrong way, but sadly he no longer has any interest.
Don't take it as him saying no—take it as the Universe
saying, "No, I have something better for you!"

Day 247: Remembering the Bad
TUESDAY

Typically, after a breakup, a woman will only remember
the good times (their first kiss) and forget all the bad times
(screaming fights). If you want to get over your ex faster, stop
excusing or romanticizing his unhealthy behavior! Force
yourself to remember all the red flags you noticed but sup-
pressed when you were dating. If necessary, make a written
list of everything that was wrong with him. For example, on
your second date, he said he forgot his wallet, asked you to
pay, and didn't pay you back. When you stayed over, he gave

you a garbage bag instead of a drawer to put your stuff in.
Should we go on?

Day 248: Bitter or Better
WEDNESDAY

A woman contacted us after her boyfriend broke up with
her and said it devastated her to find out that he immediately started dating someone else. She realized after reading
our books that she didn't follow any rules, but still couldn't
believe he would move on so quickly. She told us she was so
consumed with hatred for him she couldn't even think about
dating. We told her to change her thoughts, that she was
either going to be bitter or better. After nine months of releasing her hateful feelings and going on dates, she felt better and
met another man who was perfect for her. The next time she
ran into her ex, she was engaged and felt nothing for him!

Day 249: More Bad
THURSDAY

When you miss him, pull out your list of everything that was
wrong with him. Remember when he changed your Saturday night date to Tuesday lunch because of a "family crisis"?
You later found out that the crisis was that his ex-girlfriend
had two tickets to a Broadway show! Remember that after
the first month of courtship, he rarely planned dates, preferring to be "spontaneous," which meant home-cooked
meals and Netflix? When you asked why his ex-girlfriend
was still texting him, he screamed, "Why are you looking

at my phone?" or "You're crazy!" or "You're paranoid!" A
real charmer!

Day 250: Heartbreaker
FRIDAY

Sometimes a man who is not in love will actually break up
with you the week before Valentine's Day to avoid the holiday
altogether. This is the biggest insult, along with men who
break up with you on your birthday or New Year's. Don't get
mad or try to talk him out of it. He is making a statement,
and you need to listen. He's done, not interested. He doesn't
want to celebrate anything with you. You can text back "No
worries" or ignore him. Don't post sad stuff on social media
to get attention or sympathy. Post pretty photos and put your
profile up on dating apps to help you move on!

Day 251: Stop Thinking You'll Never Meet Anyone
SATURDAY

When a woman is getting over an ex, she usually feels that
there is only one man in the world (him). She will even
ask us, "Was he my soulmate? Am I never getting another
chance at love?" She feels loss, not to mention hysteria and
hopelessness, all *Lower Self* thoughts. We assure her that there
is more than one soulmate for everyone (he wasn't it) and that
she needs to change her thinking from lack to abundance
(*Higher Self*). We remind her that women go through breakups all the time and when they finally meet Mr. Right, they
realize why their ex was not right for them!

Day 252: Ex Factor

SUNDAY

If a guy (or even a girlfriend) breaks up with you without explanation (ghosting), don't ask why or say, "I thought we had a connection. Was I wrong?" or "Even if it's over, can you tell me what happened for my own growth, self-improvement, and next relationship?" First of all, it may have nothing to do with you. Second, you don't know if he or she will tell you the truth. Third, it's being desperate. Rules Girls don't ask or beg—we move on because knowing rarely changes the outcome anyway. Fourth, the truth could be devastating. A woman asked a guy why he ended the relationship, and he said, "I'm looking for the opposite of you." Ouch!

Apply *The Rules* to Achieve Your Higher Self

1   When you are pining over an ex, remember you're living in the past and what could have been. Live in the present, while doing one or two things to make your future brighter, whether it's buying new makeup or signing up for singles tennis lessons.

2   Keep a list of the meanest things your ex said ("I wish I never met you" or "You're insane just like your mother") on your phone or Post-its and pull it out every time you have fond feelings for him.

3   When the urge to know why an ex or friend ghosted you, tell yourself "It's none of my business," "It doesn't matter," and "Curiosity killed the cat!"

WEEK NINE
After The Ex

Your *Rules* Weekly Pep Talk

You can love again, and there is hope to find another love of your life after Mr. Right becomes your ex. Some people can get through the five stages of grief, (denial, anger, bargaining, depression, and finally, acceptance) in a week, while others take much longer. Allow yourself to mourn the loss of the person and all the lost hopes and goals you dreamed to have with them.

Part of the mourning process is letting go. Part of that struggle may be to let go of gifts, personal items, or other belongings you shared. And similar to everyone who seems to be cleaning out their closets and drawers and other clutter thanks to Marie Kondo, author of *The Life-Changing Magic of Tidying Up*, consider what to do about relationship clutter. Are you holding onto your ex's cards, gifts, letters, emails, DVDs, restaurant matchbooks, college sweatshirt, and other mementos? Don't! That's keeping your romantic partner present in your life. Throw everything out so you have a clean break. Out of sight, out of mind.

This week, focus on decluttering your ex in every way and stop talking about him so you can make room for a new Mr. Right!

AFTER THE EX

Daily *Rules*

Day 253: Stop Talking about Your Ex

MONDAY

If you want to get over your ex, stop talking about him and tell everyone you know to change the subject. Women will typically tell anyone who will listen about their breakup. They will go over all their mistakes to figure out where it went wrong and possibly salvage the relationship. They get advice from their astrologist, manicurist, therapist, trainer, hair colorist, and guy friends, hoping to crack the case. Getting rid of an ex-obsession means making a decision that it's over and done with and there's no going back. Talking about him is keeping him alive. Not talking about him will help you feel like it's dead.

Day 254: Imaginary Exes

TUESDAY

Women can get attached quickly to men they barely know. One client got stalled for a year on a guy she had only one date with. During the year, he messaged her for months but never asked her out again. We call these imaginary exes. We remind them that messages mean nothing and that it's not a genuine relationship until there are many months of consecutive Saturday night dates. *The Rules* are truth serum that suggest questions to ask so you can become more rational about how you see your relationships. What would you tell a friend who was obsessed with a guy who texted but never asked her out? Exactly! So pretend you are that friend and don't waste time on fantasy exes.

Day 255: Last Thing on Your Mind

WEDNESDAY

Of course, the last thing a woman wants to talk about after a breakup is going to singles events or posting her online profile. Even if she does go out or online, she doesn't think now is the right time. She wants to take a few months or a year to heal, so she doesn't risk a rebound relationship. She wants to listen to every podcast on breakups first. You never hear of guys waiting to date. No, they're chatting up the next girl at a bar the same night they broke up with you! If you need more motivation to move on fast, think about your ex-boyfriend talking to another girl right now!

Day 256: Tell Everyone to Cut You Off

THURSDAY

You know how a bartender will cut off a customer who is drinking too much? Ditto with getting over an ex. If you are obsessed with your ex, tell yourself and everyone you know to cut you off the second you talk about him. Don't think that talking about him is therapeutic anymore. After a certain point, it becomes addictive and destructive, not to mention boring to everyone who knows your story. A woman getting over an ex can literally talk about him all day. She's like a runaway train. Just when you thought she was over talking about him, she has one more theory on the breakup that she forgot to mention, one more insight that she thinks will shed light on the whole situation, one final piece of the puzzle that needs to be discussed, one critical plan that needs to be executed, one more conversation that needs to be had with him or his mother or sister or best friend or roommate or therapist, one more accidental running into him scenario that needs to be worked out (that's stalking), one more text or email that needs to be sent, one more item of his that she needs to return or item of hers that she must get back ASAP. It's endless and futile and sad. So ask everyone to cut you off and take you out to a bar, or singles event, or party so you get out of your head and into reality . . . and maybe meet someone new!

Day 257: Don't Be Delusional

FRIDAY

Hoping your ex will return is not only a waste of time, but often leads to depression, anxiety, and an inability to focus on work, interests, and other relationships. You tell yourself, "I know he wants to be with me but has commitment issues. I know he will eventually come around. Maybe I should send him another text." Are you ready to stop pining over your ex and living your life? Women who obsess over their exes are living in the past, frozen in time. They are in a state of unconsciousness. They are sleepwalking. To be alive is to release the old and embrace the new! If you add up all the time, energy, and money on therapists and psychics or pin-ing over an ex, you could have met someone new and been married already. A divorced client was heartbroken about a widower she dated for three months who told her he couldn't commit because he missed his wife too much. The truth is, she messaged him first on a dating app, and his wife had been dead for twenty years. This client told us she read *The Rules* backwards and forwards but couldn't wait any longer for the right man to contact her, so she took matters into her own hands. He told her he was still grieving and just looking for something casual. She suggested couples counseling and a bereavement therapist. He said no. She talked about him for a year to anyone who would listen, saying how terrible it was that he couldn't get over his grief and suspected that his dead wife was casting a spell on him. She hated his wife for keeping them apart and even went to a medium to break the bond between him and his late wife. We told her that there was no such spell and that he just wasn't interested, as he didn't message her first. Perhaps she wasn't his look and type. We advised her to pour all her energy into buying a new wardrobe, dressing up, going to singles events, posting new photos on dating apps, never contacting a man first, and stopping talking about him or seeing mediums. She felt like she was going to die because the ex-withdrawal was so great, but she was desperate to get married and listened to our advice. Six months later, she met another guy who spoke to her first, and she is now engaged.

Day 258: Throw It Out

SATURDAY

Get rid of everything sentimental he ever gave you: cards, e-mails, photos, trinkets, books, perfume, candles, and anything that reminds you of him! Unfriend him on Facebook and unfollow him on Instagram, Twitter, and other social media. You don't want to see that he announced the breakup or see status updates of him looking happily single or with his new girlfriend. Finding out that he moved on quickly could send you into a depression! If he suggests staying friends, ignore him or say "No thanks." You're the prize! You're not interested in consolation prizes!

Day 259: Skip the Angry Letters

SUNDAY

Don't send texts or handwritten letters telling your ex how much he hurt you or berate him for his alleged infidelities. It's like talking to the dead. You won't get anywhere. One woman wrote to her ex-boyfriend, "I am very sad that you are not being truthful about the text messages I found from your coworker. You were clearly living a double life for the last six months that we were together. Did you ever love me or mean anything you said? I hope she hurts you as much as you've hurt me. You deserve each other!" He never wrote back! Women should share this kind of letter with a dating coach or therapist, not an ex. Most men will not respond or even acknowledge it.

Apply *The Rules* to Achieve Your Higher Self

1   Throw out your ex's stuff, such as cards or concert ticket stubs.

2   Every time you have a Hallmark-movie-type memory about your ex, immediately switch it to a terrible fight you had. Practice the law of substitution.

3   If you've been writing emails or handwritten letters to your ex, either delete, burn, or discuss them with your dating coach or therapist. Don't send anything to him!

WEEK TEN
Self-Examination and Second Chances

Your *Rules* Weekly Pep Talk

Breakups offer an opportunity for self-examination and second chances. You might be obsessed with all the what-ifs and could-haves. The last thing on your mind is looking at yourself and what you might have done differently—you just want your happy Hollywood ending. You just want him to call and say he made the biggest mistake of his life and run over with flowers and take-out food.

While waiting for your ex to come back or a new man to walk into your life, we suggest writing or telling a *Rules*-y friend about any mistakes you made that contributed to the breakup, such as being mean or complaining from your *Lower Self's* perspective. And then let it go. Ruminating over what you could have done or should have done will not serve you or empower you, but vowing to do *The Rules* next time will!

This week, focus on being your *Higher Self*, starting with some soul-searching and committing to being easier to be with going forward. This is why we always recommend a childhood dating history consultation, which clarifies what part you played in the breakup.

SELF-EXAMINATION AND SECOND CHANCES
Daily *Rules*

Day 260: Self-Examination
MONDAY

When a client calls us about an ex, we often find that it is
not her first breakup or first non-*Rules* relationship. This is
why we always recommend a childhood and dating history
to uncover patterns of self-sabotaging behavior or character
traits that must be rooted out to recover from this breakup
and prevent the next one. As Plato famously said, "An unex-
amined life is not worth living." Self-examination applies to
dating! We strongly suggest looking at any personality short-
comings that contributed to the breakup—for example, acting insecure or pushy, suggesting more couple time, or trying
to change him.

Day 261: Don't Publicly Bad-Mouth Your Ex
TUESDAY

"Hell hath no fury like a woman scorned" means that no one
is angrier than a woman who has been rejected or cheated
on. You're so angry that you may feel like bad-mouthing
your ex on social media. One client told us that when her
boyfriend ended their relationship on her birthday, she
wanted to post on Instagram, "Birthday breakup! Really?"
She also wanted to quote Maya Angelou, "When someone
shows you who they are, believe them the first time!" We
told her no, because she would come across as hurt and like

a victim. The most effective way to get even is not to throw a pity party, but an actual party and post that.

Day 262: Don't Become Obsessed

WEDNESDAY

Before you were obsessed with your ex-boyfriend, you were the most unselfish person. Now you're forgetting your friends' birthdays and being self-absorbed. Your mother and friends and coworkers can't listen anymore. They let your calls go into voicemail. You have psychics, therapists, dating coaches, and healers on speed dial to go over the relationship just in case you missed something! They have already helped you stalk him, follow him on social media, and find out if he has a new girlfriend and what gym he belongs to. They have nothing left to give and feel used. Let him go, then go back to being a good friend!

Day 263: Bad Karma

THURSDAY

Don't waste your time plotting revenge. Most women are understandably angry after a breakup and want to hurt their ex or make him regret his decision. We remind them that they should not want what they can't have and love only those who love them. We tell them that wishing their ex ill is unkind karma and a bad use of their time and energy. We suggest they work on forgiveness and releasing any bitterness, as it will only boomerang! If you really want to hurt your ex, meet and marry someone else!

Day 264: Running into Him

FRIDAY

Some women who have been broken up with plot to *accidentally* run into their exes. They frequent restaurants in his area or pretend to walk their dog in his neighborhood. Any ex who sees you in his area will know that you're stalking him. Don't do it. Even if you run into him "accidentally," it will not make him say, "Why don't we grab coffee or get back together?" He has your number. He knows how to reach you. Your life isn't a romantic comedy where you can make things magically happen or force a reconciliation by just showing up. The energy you're using (begging family and friends to drive with you to his area) should go to singles events or cool bars!

Day 265: Breakthrough

SATURDAY

A breakup can actually be a breakthrough, as long as you don't fight it. It's the resistance to the breakup, not so much the breakup itself, that's the problem. Most women approach an unwanted breakup with a big no: "This can't be happening. He made a mistake. I have to get him back. He's the only one for me, and I'll figure out a way to change his mind . . ." instead of thinking, "This is for my Higher Good, this is exactly what I need, and if he was The One, he wouldn't have ended it and we would still be together." Your *Lower Self* will resist the truth. Your *Higher Self* will embrace it.

DAY 266: If You Spot It
SUNDAY

If something bothers you a lot about your ex or any other person, then you must have or have had that quality in the past because it wouldn't bother you otherwise. As the saying goes, "If you spot it, you got it." Instead of feeling hate or anger towards that person, just see yourself in them and practice forgiveness or tolerance. If someone's being really mean, resist the urge to hate them back (*Lower Self*). Realize that they themselves are hurt people, and if they're being mean, they can't be happy. Try to feel sorry for them because what happy person would be so mean? Treat the person with compassion, like a patient in a hospital, but at a distance. Don't be a glutton for punishment. Pray for them, but stay away from them!

Apply *The Rules* to Achieve Your Higher Self

1 Self-examination is an ancient practice. Whether you do it because you're broken up with or as a New Year's resolution, resolve today to look at yourself and do better!

2 Some women feel that they're too old to change their bad dating habits. Not true! As long as your heart is beating, there's hope. Make one change today. Don't text your ex to ask if you can get back together!

3 If you want to make your ex regret the breakup, go to parties and out with other guys and post photos on social media. Busy, busy!

COURSE 5

Create
Respectful
Marriages and
Partnerships

12 WEEKS

Hopefully, you have been practicing being your *Higher Self* in all your relationships because it will definitely come in handy when you're married. Some marriages can be easy because you married your best friend and are on the same page with just about everything. You're both neat freaks, early risers, and gym rats, and you both like Chinese food, sitcoms, making up quickly, and staying home on Saturday night. In other marriages, while you love each other to pieces, you're complete opposites, and you have to be the better person to make it work.

For example, you knew your lawyer husband was ambitious, but you did not know he was going to run for political office. He's campaigning nights and weekends, and you feel like a single mother raising your three kids. You're not into politics and care more about what he's doing at home than in your hometown. You're angry all the time and feel sorry for yourself. "I didn't sign up for this!" You feel if he loved you, he would give up politics and be a more involved husband and father.

Every married client has some variation of this theme. For example, "I knew he liked to make investments, but I had no idea he would put money into some crazy risky stock. I'm furious he put us in this situation," or "I knew he wasn't a cuddler, but I never thought he would fall asleep in his recliner watching sports some nights. I feel single going to bed alone. How is this a marriage?" or "No matter how much I do, my husband always has some criticism disguised as a suggestion, like 'You almost hit our neighbor's car, don't forget to straighten the steering wheel when you park.' God forbid he ever gave me a compliment. I work and take care of the house and two small kids. Each time he says something I feel hurt, and then he tells me I'm *too sensitive*. I can't win!" or "I'm angry that I'm the breadwinner. We made about the same amount of money when we met, then he lost his job and found a job making less. He's gotten very comfortable letting me carry the load. I don't think he's ever emptied the dishwasher. How is this fair?"

In every situation, we try to explain that marriage is *for better, for worse, for richer, for poorer* and that you can't change your spouse (we're sure you tried), so you might as well become a positive and valuable member of your family team. Maybe look at it as free coaching or that he's just trying to be helpful, instead of criticism.

Sometimes you do more or earn more income, and sometimes he does more or is the breadwinner. It always evens out in the end. We're sure some politicians' wives were not thrilled either, but the happily married ones threw their hats in the ring instead of complaining. If you can't beat him, join him. It takes less energy to play the game than fight him!

We help our clients learn that they can't make a workaholic not check his emails on vacation any more than they can make a slackard more motivated. You can't make a husband who likes to fall asleep with the remote control on ESPN cuddle watching rom-coms with you. That's not realistic. You have to respect his lifestyle and choices, as you would want him to respect that you like to watch the *Real Housewives* shows, and not try to make him a carbon copy of you. Acting like you are being put upon and walking around with self-righteous anger is going to make you miserable or divorced.

We find that the married clients who complain always find something to complain about. He works too much or too little. He spends too much, or he's cheap. He doesn't take care of himself, or he's at the gym all weekend. It's so much easier to surrender and say, "Okay, this is my husband. I love him, and I married him. All this stuff is annoying, but not a deal-breaker." It's less work in the long run to accept him, warts and all, and not be reactive. Besides, when you are so busy fuming that your husband is not around or not helpful, you have little or no time to realize your own dreams. You could start a book club or create a food blog or take up tennis in the amount of time you are noticing and commenting on his every flaw.

Your *Lower Self* loves to complain about how awful your husband is. He left his socks on the floor; he put his drink on the table without a coaster . . . oh no, call the police! Your *Higher Self* knows that everything is exactly the way it is supposed to be for your own benefit. Many married women started successful businesses because their husbands were unemployed. They were too busy creating instead of reacting. So if your husband is constantly making suggestions, instead of grumbling or getting huffy, be diplomatic and say, "Thanks, I never thought about it that way." Basically look at it like you're getting free life coaching when your husband corrects you.

Every time we tell a married client to treat her husband as the leader of the family and offer them admiration with love and respect no matter how she feels, her marriage changes for the better in ten weeks or less! Some even see results overnight. Follow *The Rules for Marriage* formula as soon as possible, as whatever you're doing now, being your burnt-up *Lower Self*, certainly isn't working!

WEEK ONE
Engaged

Your *Rules* Weekly Pep Talk

Great job! You're engaged, and all is moving along as you had hoped. We want to caution you that being engaged doesn't mean the end of *The Rules*. It means making minor adjustments in how you interact and communicate with your fiancé. Don't fall into a false sense of security just because you got the ring. You need to continue using *The Rules* both before and after you are married.

When you are in the honeymoon phase of your engagement, we recommend your fiancé should still do most of the calling and texting, planning, and paying, but now that you're planning a wedding, you obviously can talk to him and see him more often, maybe three or four times a week instead of two.

This week, focus on keeping your independence and spending the majority of your time on work, family, friends, interests, and the gym while enjoying this engagement phase of becoming future lifelong partners.

ENGAGED
Daily *Rules*

Day 267: Love at First Sight

MONDAY

If he says, after a year or more of dating, that he's not sure how he feels, don't believe him. Men know right away how they feel and if you're The One. In some of the longest-lasting marriages, the man said, "That's the woman I'm going to marry," based on knowing her for ten minutes. Fashion designer Tom Ford said, upon meeting his partner of thirty-five years in an elevator: "You're The One. That's it. Click. Sold. It was literally love at first sight." So if he says he needs more time, say, "Okay, call me when you know," and then stop seeing him and date other people.

Day 268: Don't Spoil the Proposal

TUESDAY

Your boyfriend said he's going to propose around the holidays. If he doesn't, do you say anything on the spot? We think not because that would ruin the holiday weekend! Your *Lower Self* wants to say, "Hey, what's going on?" but your *Higher Self* knows to be poised and patient! He forgot, you forgot! Don't worry, he's not getting away with anything. The next time he asks to see you, say, "I can't see you anymore without a proposal." A client was skiing with her boyfriend, who had mentioned proposing by New Year's. She was texting us from the mountain, ready to blow up. We told her not

to. Of course, he proposed two minutes later with a ring he
had in his jacket pocket.

Day 269: Marry Me!
FRIDAY

In a recent op-ed article in the *Los Angeles Times*, a sociologist
asked why women can't propose, claiming that men proposing
is an archaic tradition. While that may sound good in theory,
letting everyone be equal, we believe it makes the woman
the aggressor and the man passive, which doesn't work in
romantic relationships. It's upending the natural order of
things, which is that men love to lead and love a challenge.
It's making women become the more interested party and, as
in life as in love, the less interested party wins! It's the woman
chasing the man, which will make her feel insecure, especially
if he says no. She'll always wonder if he was going to do it first,
or ever. If a man doesn't propose, she can simply ask where
the relationship is going and then she'll have her answer, but
no need to ask his hand in marriage . . . ever! Will she buy
the ring and get down on bended knee? Where will all this
pseudo-equality end? In the same article, the sociologist said
most women said they would be embarrassed to propose, and
most men said they want to do the proposing.

Day 270: Don't Be a Diva
WEDNESDAY

Now that you've got the ring and the wedding date, does
that mean you throw *The Rules* out the window? No, you

still need to follow *The Rules for Engagement*. You still don't see him twenty-four seven. If you live together, don't be needy or glued to his side. Be independent and stay in your power. While planning the wedding, don't be a diva, and be nice to his family and friends. Perhaps you want an elaborate affair, he wants something low-key, or vice versa. Don't demand that everything go your way. Some brides are so obsessed with the perfect party that they forget to include their fiancé in the decision-making. Of course, if he's fine with you picking the flowers, venue, and everything else, great, but if he wants to be involved, let him. Posting pretty photos on Facebook and Instagram is not the goal—being happily married is. We know it's hard if your whole life you've dreamed of a big fancy wedding but your fiancé would rather spend the money on the down payment for a house. Don't throw a fit or mope around complaining that he's being cheap. You can still have a beautiful wedding on a small budget. Send e-vites instead of fancy invitations, hire a DJ instead of a live band, use candles instead of expensive floral centerpieces, wear a simple slip dress instead of something poofy and pricey, have a buffet instead of a sit-down dinner, and ask your friends to take photos and videos instead of hiring a photographer. Better to get along with your future husband and buy a house for a lifetime than blow the same money in five hours. And of course, many details can go wrong with even the best wedding planning, so try not to be a bridezilla!

Day 271: Lay Low
THURSDAY

If you're engaged, lay low and don't flash your ring in a friend's face or post incessantly on social media, assuming that they will be happy for you. Some people, even close friends who are still single, may not be able to take the good news. Unless they are your BFF and your good news is their good news, better that someone else tell them or they read about it online. When talking to insecure, jealous, or not the happiest or depressed friends, try to downplay it if it comes up at all or preferably tell them about your bad back or other problems. Social media has made weddings more competitive. Everyone wants to post the perfect venue, six-tiered cake, daddy-daughter dance, designer wedding dress with long train and tiara, five-inch Manolo Blahnik heels, heartwarming vows, and charming toasts. Before you get caught up in all the photo ops, remind yourself that getting along with your husband before, during, and after the wedding is more important than how everything looks on Facebook and Instagram. Not sharing isn't lying. This is being a good, thoughtful friend. It's being your *Higher Self*, putting their feelings before your own. This is like dating— being honest but mysterious. If you've found your soulmate and your friend can't get a second date, they might be a tad jealous. It's human nature. If you want to keep friends, don't brag from your *Lower Self*.

Day 272: Take the High Ground

SATURDAY

A client's dream guy proposed. She wanted Whitney Houston's upbeat "I Wanna Dance with Somebody" as her wedding song. Her husband wanted something more subdued, but meaningful: "All I Ask of You" from Andrew Lloyd Webber's *The Phantom of the Opera*. She called all her bridesmaids, and most of them took her side because they wanted to dance. She and her husband argued about it, and she contacted us. We told her you can play dancing music all night, but your wedding song should have more weight and depth than disco. "Anywhere you go, let me go too / Love me, that's all I ask of you." If your husband cares so much to choose something so heartfelt, go along with him.

Day 273: Focus on What Matters Most

SUNDAY

In general, we believe in taking a husband's last name, as it's traditional and *The Rules* are traditional. But it's an individual decision, which is why we offer private consultations to discuss the pros and cons. Sometimes a client wants to keep her maiden name or hyphenate it with her husband's last name because of her career or because she loves her father who only has daughters and wants to keep her last name going. Others want to keep their maiden name because they are celebrities, VIPs, or authors. However, Jennifer Lopez decided to take Ben Affleck's last name because it's "traditional" and "romantic." What if your partner asks you for a prenup? Rules Girls are not gold diggers, so we have no problem signing a prenup. But if she has more money, she can ask him to sign her prenup. We don't believe that money is a big factor in a *Rules* marriage. You both married for love, for richer or poorer, so it's not a deal-breaker.

Apply *The Rules* to Achieve Your Higher Self

1 *The Rules* still apply even at your own wedding. Let your husband find you in the crowd and ask you to dance.

2 When you want to blow the budget, remember it's more important to be happily married than to have an Instagram-perfect wedding. Marriage is about compromise.

3 When you're engaged, don't be a bridezilla. Also, try to be sensitive and helpful to single friends who haven't been so lucky in love.

All Committed Relationships Need *The Rules*

Your *Rules* Weekly Pep Talk

The Rules not only work for dating, romantic partners, and
husbands, but for various other committed relationships you
have in your life. If you're the type of person who thinks she
has the answers for everyone (if only so- and- so did this or
so- and- so did that, everything would be wonderful), remind
yourself that you are not a relationship expert. This is when
you need to pull back and realize that no one's asking for
your advice. It sounds altruistic to want to save the world, but
it can also be intrusive if no one is asking!

This week, focus on waiting to be asked for help from
everyone in every area of your life, including waiting for
those on social media to contact you first. Remember, the
road to hell is paved with good intentions. Giving unsolicited
advice can be misconstrued as meddling and also takes away
precious time that could be spent on yourself. As spiritual
leader Emmet Fox said, "Those who mind other people's
business always neglect their own." What are you neglecting
in your own life? Do that and leave everyone else alone!

ALL COMMITTED RELATIONSHIPS NEED *THE RULES*
Daily *Rules*

Day 274: *Rules* for Friends
MONDAY

Even with the best of intentions, chances are you will ruin a relationship if you give unsolicited advice. If you say to a girl-friend, "Hey, I've noticed you're always hooking up and get-ting hurt. Boy, do I have a book for you!" She may not take it well. She should call you and ask you for help, based on the way you date and live. When you call her, you could possibly catch her at a bad time and get a cold shoulder, like when you call a guy who is watching a ball game and he gets off the phone first. Ouch! Wait for women to ask for your advice like you wait for men to ask you out!

Day 275: *Rules* for Buyer Beware People
TUESDAY

You probably think that Buyer Beware only applies to men. Not so! Anyone, including family members, friends, and people you work with, can be Buyer Beware people if they are only or primarily interested in you in order to get something. Maybe they want to meet your cute brother, social climb (you know someone famous or belong to a country club), have you fix their computer, write their resume, or act like their therapist. It's not mutual. Their motives are not pure, and if you didn't help them with whatever, you wouldn't hear from them that much! Buyer

Beware . . . Next! Love only those who love you and
don't use you!

Day 276: *Rules* for Coworkers
WEDNESDAY

Do you feel your coworker is taking advantage of you? Your
boss put you on a project with her, but you're doing most
of the work. She takes long lunches, and that annoys you
because you eat a sandwich at your desk to get more work
done. You want to have "a few words" with her, but you're
stuck because your boss likes her. Do you have a history of
watching what other people do and getting mad? We believe,
do your work and go home—don't be a bean counter or a
martyr and don't care too much. Life is a long road. You
never know when she'll help you out or put in a good word.
Or just get another job!

Day 277: *Rules* for Work
THURSDAY

Relationships at work can be challenging. There may be
difficult personalities to deal with, mean bosses, nepotism,
office gossips, backstabbers, and slackers. Do *The Rules*
at work by keeping your head down and not talking to
anyone first, unless it is absolutely necessary. Anything you
need to know or do will be told to you. It's always a better
conversation when your boss or coworker talks to you first!
If you have an idea, suggest it once. Be a team player, not
the star. Stay out of company drama and watercooler gossip.

Go to work, do your best, and go home! But what if you work for yourself (say, a life coach or tutor) and you feel taken advantage of by clients who haggle over money or go over their time? One coach told us she gave three hours to a client and only charged her for one! She was resentful and burnt out. We asked, "Whose fault is that?" Remember, you're in charge of setting boundaries and prices, so don't be a people-pleaser. Treat work and clients like dating or like a therapist and say, "So sorry, but you are out of time." They won't respect your time if you don't!

Day 278: *Rules* for Bosses

FRIDAY

Sometimes clients ask us how to deal with their disrespectful bosses. We tell them that while they can't make a mean boss nicer, their livelihood depends on making them happy, so try to be useful and stay out of his or her line of fire. One of our single clients is a ghostwriter for a wealthy publisher who swears a lot. She asked us what we thought of telling him to put twenty dollars in a swear jar every time he cursed. We said, "No, you work for him. He doesn't work for you. Don't try to penalize him—don't you need to pay your rent? Unfortunately, you will need to walk away or ignore the swear words until you find another job or contact HR. In the meantime, don't take his venom personally because it has nothing to do with you" (*Higher Self*). When she stopped caring and started looking for another job, his cursing no longer bothered her.

Day 279: *Rules* for Facebook
SATURDAY

If you have a friend or relative who rarely includes you in her social plans, then don't friend her first on Facebook or follow her on Instagram. Try not to look at her page because seeing her smiling in photos with other people might be too much for you to bear. Some women do the opposite and force themselves into being Facebook friends. They think, "I'll just like all her posts and make flattering comments so she'll possibly reciprocate and include me in her world." We find that that doesn't actually work, and it turns you into a groupie. Whether in real life or social media, let others like you first.

Day 280: *Rules* for Everyone
SATURDAY

If you live your life each day from your *Higher Self*, you will get along with most everyone. Be kind, thoughtful, and respectful. Treat others how you want to be treated, and others will mirror back to you how you are treating them. Be rational and walk away from anyone who does not respect or isn't nice to you. Don't participate in conversations with people who yell, talk down to you, or mistreat you. Stay in your power and stand strong when people throw angry or hurtful words at you. Don't take other people's emotions on and don't react or give your power to someone else.

Apply *The Rules* to Achieve Your Higher Self

1 When the urge comes over you to "fix" a friend who is not asking for help, fix something in your own life instead, like your broken dishwasher.

2 When you feel like telling your husband, sibling, or adult children what to do, do it yourself. There is only one way to truly help people: by example!

3 When you feel your boss doesn't appreciate you or pay you enough, think about what you can give to the company, not what you can get. Or stop making work so important or get another job.

274 The Rules Handbook

WEEK THREE
Marriage

Your *Rules* Weekly Pep Talk

Marriage can be a wonderful union if you realize you are both on the same team and working towards the same goal. That may be hard to remember when you are angry, hurt, or frustrated with your partner. Experts say people always hurt the one they love, and that could not be more true in the case of marriage.

When your feelings get hurt because you felt your husband criticized or didn't compliment you, you may want to say something mean and hurt him. But we know that taking offense and saying something unkind in response doesn't work long term. It's your *Lower Self* looking to win a useless argument with a cheap shot that may feel good in the moment but leaves you with a hangover. Once you reframe the situation and realize that maybe your husband is just trying to be helpful towards his teammate, you'll be able to respond from your *Higher Self.*

This week, focus on taking a deep breath when you feel slighted and saying something *Higher Self* like, "You may have a point," or "Thanks for sharing, I'll think about it." Light a candle instead of putting out the flame.

MARRIAGE

Daily *Rules*

Day 281: Not So Easy

MONDAY

After we wrote *The Rules*, many of our readers and clients got engaged or married and asked us for marriage advice. So we wrote *The Rules for Marriage*, which is basically the opposite of *The Rules*. You were "hard to get" to get him, and now you need to be "easy to be with" to keep him. We said let him win, don't nag, don't force him to talk, don't try to change him, say yes to intimacy, and don't use the D word (divorce), among other rules. Simple, but not easy! It's one thing to be light and breezy for a year or two of dating. It's another to be easygoing for the rest of your life, but it's worth it! Don't worry, we'll tell you exactly how to be your *Higher Self* with your husband!

Day 282: Stop Wishing

TUESDAY

A common reaction to *The Rules* and *The Rules for Marriage* is "I wish it wasn't this way. I wish I didn't have to be a challenge to get him or be a saint to keep him." We wish it wasn't this way either. We wish we could do whatever we wanted in the areas of dating and marriage, but that's a useless thought. It's like saying, "I wish I didn't have to go to college for four years," or "I wish I didn't get older." Don't say "I wish." Say "Okay, I don't like it, but how do I do it?"

Rules Girls are realists who love results. We don't create a fantasy world where anything goes and sitting around wishing works . . . it doesn't!

Day 283: Happy Husband, Happy Life
WEDNESDAY

Feminism has been great for giving women better pay and equal opportunities at work, but not so great for dating and marriage. As women became more successful in business, they also became more masculine around men and either stayed single or got married and divorced. For many women, work and money became more important than marriage, and the boardroom became more important than the bedroom. People say "Happy wife, happy life!" as if women should work and shop all day, get Botox, and audition for a *Real Housewives* show. This is not the case. It's a "happy husband, happy life." When a husband is happy, he stays. When he's unhappy, he leaves or is just miserable to be with. An empowered woman puts her husband first.

Day 284: Discovering Diplomacy
THURSDAY

Newly married women are happy, until they discover their husbands are secret hoarders (baseball cards, sneakers, broken exercise equipment). They don't want his stuff touching their pristine space. But you have to be diplomatic. If you demand that he get rid of it, he could leave with all his belongings. Ask him if he wants your help to declutter.

If not, give him a man cave or spare room or the garage to store his valuables and close the door. Don't act snobby. It's not like *Architectural Digest* is coming over. Your marriage is more important than trying to copy organizing guru Marie Kondo! Even Kondo wisely said that her home is messy and she is okay with that because spending time with her husband and three children is more important than having a perfectly tidy home. Think about that when you want to scream at your husband for leaving dirty socks on the floor and stacks of newspapers in the garage.

Day 285: On Call

FRIDAY

Being married is like being a doctor on call—your life is not your own. You had planned to put your feet up on the couch, eat popcorn in pajamas, and watch a romantic comedy, but your husband asks if it's okay to invite his brother, who just broke up with his girlfriend, over to watch a ball game. Do it! Roll out the red carpet and offer to buy the chips and beer. Don't say, "OMG, can you watch the game at a bar? I really wanted to chill. He's always breaking up and making up. I can't listen to his girlfriend drama anymore! When is he going to get married already and leave us alone?" Doing the things you don't want to do or that are inconvenient to make your husband happy will win you brownie points down the road. He will never forget it. He will do something equally kind in return one day. Kindness in marriage is like money in the bank.

Day 286: Intimacy

SATURDAY

Men and women can have very different needs when it comes
to intimacy. The more masculine partner usually determines
your intimate life. Whether they want it every night or are
not that interested, your relationship will grow deeper and
more connected if you choose to make time for intimacy. So
don't say, "I'm not in the mood." Figure out when you will
be! We're not saying to grin and bear it, but understand that
intimacy is an important part of marriage and that physical
connection often leads to emotional connection, so it's a win,
win (*Higher Self*). Tell yourself you're lucky to have a husband
who is attracted to you and wants to be with you. Discuss
when, especially if you work and have children, but try not
to say a hard no every time. Maybe you're tired, or maybe
you're just being lazy or selfish (*Lower Self*). Sometimes even
a quickie is still better than nothing. Lack of intimacy can
lead to feeling like roommates instead of lovers. Conversely,
don't force it on your husband if he's not interested. Some
women assume all men want intimacy all the time. Not true.
Some men have lower drives or are more into work or sports.
If you are more into intimacy than your husband, it's fine to
initiate in a feminine way, as long as you don't get angry if he
turns you down.

Day 287: The *Rules* Partner

SUNDAY

After the honeymoon stage, people often complain that their partners don't pay more attention to them. *Rules* wives have the opposite problem . . . they get too much attention! *Rules* partners want to do everything with them, from cooking and cleaning to going to doctors' appointments and watching TV shows and movies. These partners don't want a man cave or separate bedrooms and vacations. They're even happy to hang out with your dysfunctional family. You basically can't get rid of them. A *Rules* partner will call to tell you he got an oil change and had pizza for lunch and basically include you in every detail of his life!

Apply *The Rules* to Achieve Your Higher Self

1   When you feel hurt by your husband's insensitive sense of humor, it's natural to want to say something sarcastic back. In that moment, try to remember that the Greek definition of sarcasm is "to tear the flesh" and don't say it! When you're not feeling fond of your husband, remind yourself that he married you and you never have to date again!

2   No matter how upset you feel, don't say the D word (divorce) in an argument, as it may plant the seed for a future split. Say it enough and your husband will say it back.

3   When your husband says something you think is stupid or you don't agree with, don't say anything in the moment if you feel like you're going to fly off the handle. Two wrongs don't make a right. Practice silence!

WEEK FOUR

Marriage Is a Partnership, So Be a Team Player

Your *Rules* Weekly Pep Talk

There have been many debates about who should lead in a marriage. Ask yourself, is it about what is fair or what is effective? Every team has only one leader because it is more efficient and helpful. Each partner has their strengths and weaknesses. It's best to focus on the strengths before deciding who is most qualified to make the decision. This does not mean you do not have a voice or can't share what you prefer; it just means that you recognize the most effective way to make the decision is if you let him take the lead.

Masculine energy partners prefer to be more direct and in charge, while feminine partners tend to be more nurturing. This isn't absolute. Whatever your situation, focus on being a valuable team player and more agreeable instead of argumentative and see how well it works. Of course, we advise our readers to pick their battles. Let him win things that are less important to you, like what restaurant you are going to for New Year's Eve or where you're going on vacation, so you can negotiate harder for things like hiring a cleaning lady or donating to charity you love.

This week, be more agreeable instead of argumentative and see how well it works. The more actions you take to create a harmonious partnership, the happier you both will be.

MARRIAGE IS A PARTNERSHIP, SO BE A TEAM PLAYER
Daily *Rules*

Day 288: Is Your Partner the Primary Decision-Maker?

MONDAY

There are many books and theories about marriage, so we're going to make this really simple for you because if it's not simple, you will not remember it, much less do it! Your husband or partner may want to be the decision-maker of your relationship. We know it sounds sexist and anti-feminist, but it's the truth. Just like dating isn't 100% equal (the guy has to pursue you and propose), marriage isn't always either. So if you both agree, your husband or partner is the decision-maker and you are his key supportive team member . . . even if you make the same amount of money or more. That's because romantic relationships are based on biology, not finance. There's a hierarchy that goes back to caveman days. If you act too bossy or overbearing, you will emasculate your husband and your marriage will suffer. So, let him take the lead role as the decision-maker.

Day 289: Not Kidding

TUESDAY

You are probably thinking, "You've got to be kidding," and that we are asking you to be a Stepford wife. Don't worry, we're not! Stepford wives are robots without brains. You have a brain and a personality. You just have to be feminine, not masculine, by doing *The Rules for Marriage*. We are feminists and believe women can do whatever they want, except with men. We can run a business, climb the corporate ladder, train for a marathon, buy a condo, and even run for President of the Condo Board Association or President of the United States. But we have to defer to our husbands and not treat them like coworkers or girlfriends because it doesn't work! The majority of men like to feel that they are in control!

Day 290: Empowered Partner
WEDNESDAY

Before the 1970s, most women prided themselves on being great homemakers. It was a noble and respectable position in the family. Now, to feel worthy, women have to be the best worker, the best mother, the best yoga devotee, the best PTA member, the best Facebook friend, the best 5K runner, and the best fundraiser. Those are a lot of roles to play and be the leader of. Take a deep breath and decide where and when to use your valuable energy. Choose your battles carefully and where to invest your time and energy. You might ask, "Why do I have to give up some of my power at home when my partner already married me?" and in many cases, "I know how to do things better!" Marriage is a dance of the masculine and feminine. Let the masculine lead on the dance floor of marriage so you don't stumble over each other.

Day 291: Sure!

Once you see that marriage is not always 100% equal in every area, your relationship will become easier. Sometimes you may feel like you're carrying a heavier load. Try not to keep track of every favor or sacrifice you've made and expect your offerings to be returned someday. This expectation will just be exhausting, causing you to become weary and unfortunately, vengeful. So if he asks, "Can you do this errand?" or "Let's visit my parents this weekend," or "Don't spend money this month—work is slow," or whatever, your *Higher Self* will choose to be a team player and say "Sure!" If he requests a prenup, there must be a good reason, and if you love him, you will understand. If he doesn't want a joint account, don't. If he says no to a sleep-away camp because money is tight, even though all of your friends are sending their kids away, agree. If he wants more intimacy, try to agree. If he says he's too tired to be intimate, don't nag him to do it. Therefore, there are no fights because you're a team player.

Day 292: Be on the Saint Plan

Be supportive and a team player with whatever your situation is, be it financial, medical, or emotional and with stepchildren, ex-wives, and so on. You will *never* win the marriage game by having wars with your mean in-laws, complaining about his kids from his previous marriage, or coaching him about his career, weight, beer buddies, or baseball card collection. Forget it! Successfully married women know who they are married to and try not to argue. Do you think Kate Middleton told Prince William that she didn't want to visit the Queen or pose for Buckingham Palace or *People* magazine photographers? We don't think so! Learn from her as a positive role model.

Day 293: Not Fair

SATURDAY

Okay, so you're probably thinking this is so unfair. You probably have a lot of pet peeves. "Why do I have to do so much work in my marriage? Why do I have to watch every penny while he wastes it on football tickets? Why do I have to pick up his dry cleaning when we both work eight-hour days? So I do all this work for *what*? So I have to be his cheerleader and put him first before friends and work for *what*?" For the privilege of staying married! For no divorce lawyers! For no custody battles! For security! For growing old together! Just do it—it works! It's less work in the long run.

Day 294: Curb Your Enthusiasm

SUNDAY

Men usually initiate intimacy, but what if you're the one with the higher physical drive? Should you suggest it? We think occasionally, as in "rarely return his calls" when dating. If your husband is a workaholic or is fine with being intimate once a week, leave him alone. You would prefer it three times a week, but you don't always get what you want. Don't be the aggressor in the physical department. Asking a husband who is tired to be intimate may be asking too much. Of course you can initiate anything, but do so at your own risk, as he might say, "Not tonight, honey," and you might feel hurt! It's always better when he's in the mood!

Apply *The Rules* to Achieve Your Higher Self

1   It's okay to try to gently change cosmetic things about your husband, like his clothes or hairstyle, if he lets you, but don't try to change his essence. For example, don't tell him not to watch sports or go to the gym.

2   Every time you think "I do so much," think of all the thankless manly things he does like changing the tires, taking out the garbage, and cleaning the grill.

3   When you come home from work where you have a fancy title like Senior VP of Corporate Marketing and Investor Relations and run a staff of fifty people, switch from masculine to feminine mode. Set the table, cook dinner, and ask him nicely to help clean up!

WEEK FIVE
Effective Marriage Communication

Your *Rules* Weekly Pep Talk

When you can effectively communicate with your marriage partner, your home life will run smoothly. Marriage has more to do with your mindset than your circumstances. When your *Higher Self* focuses on the many things you could be grateful for and you cheer each other on every day, then the odds of finding a "win-win" solution in your daily battles will increase.

Married women often think, "If only I had more money, more childcare, more vacations, then I would be happy." The reality is, you can have all of those things and still want more or fight about your vacation or whine about all the things you don't have, instead of being thankful for what you do have. Gratitude is key to creating a happy marriage.

Emmet Fox tells a story about helping people with emotional problems and depression. He stated that he enjoyed working with wealthy people the most. Why? Not because they could pay his fee or make a large donation. Working with the wealthy actually saved him many, many hours of treatment because these clients already knew that money didn't solve their problems. They were rich and still had problems. This allowed Fox to get straight to the source of the problem without the client resisting. So many times, people come in for help thinking, "If I could just have $1,000, I could solve my problem and be happy again." Fox says,

"Money doesn't solve problems," and the wealthy already
know that.

This week, focus on being happy you married the person
you wanted and that you are blessed with so many wonderful experiences and memories with him every day, regardless
of your financial situation or how you feel about what is not
going your way. If you're not out there dating again, you're
having a good married life!

EFFECTIVE MARRIAGE COMMUNICATION
Daily *Rules*

Day 295: Change Yourself, Not Your Partner
MONDAY

The institution of marriage was not created to make you happy all the time. Committed relationships with others are meant to bring out our *Higher Self.* Change your thoughts, not your husband, and you will have a happier marriage. Everybody wants their husbands to change, but nobody wants to change themselves or their attitude. Changing other people without changing yourself is an exercise in futility and a waste of time! If you think your marriage is good and your husband is a good guy (faithful, goes to work, plays sports with the kids), then count your blessings!

Day 296: Stop Complaining
TUESDAY

Sometimes married clients complain their husband isn't handier around the house ("I do everything"), doesn't spend more time with their children ("I feel like a single mom"), doesn't have the best bedside manner ("He was talking to his boss while driving me to surgery"), or screws up their supermarket order ("I said organic!"). It's easy to expect your husband to be more helpful or thoughtful or the Father of the Year, but how would you feel if he wasn't there at all? When you feel annoyed by him, pause and try to remember that no one was helping you before you were married (your roommate and parents don't count). Don't compare him to Superman—compare him to no one and appreciate all that he does.

Day 297: Let Your Partner Be Right

WEDNESDAY

If you want to be happily married, let your husband be right. We're not saying he's actually always right, but see the situation from his point of view. Let him win some battles and save your energy for the big issues. For example, a client's husband told her, "You left the refrigerator door open while you were cutting vegetables." Instead of just closing the door, she felt it necessary to say, "Well, sometimes you leave it open too, and I don't tell you." He got defensive, and they bickered about who does what. Then when he left the refrigerator door open the next day, she triumphantly pointed it out, and he said, "You don't have to rub it in." If she had just closed the refrigerator door and not said anything, he would not have been so angry. But her *Lower Self* was at work. She wanted to win a useless argument and, of course, regretted it. Don't be childish and pick your battles!

Day 298: Don't Be Defensive

THURSDAY

A client's husband complained she was rude to the nanny. She told him, "Maybe you're putting me down to make yourself feel better because you didn't get that promotion." Playing armchair psychologist made him angrier. "No, it's because you were rude." She continued to defend herself, and they didn't speak all weekend. We advised her to say, "You may have a point." If you want to get along with your husband, consider it might be the truth and don't get defensive. We did a childhood and dating history consultation with this client, and guess what, several ex-boyfriends, bosses, and roommates also found her rude! We told her to work on that!

Day 299: Wording

FRIDAY

Some people say, "It's not what you say, it's how you say it." We believe, "It's what you say and how you say it." Don't tell your husband, "I can't believe you forgot our anniversary." Say "I'd love to celebrate our anniversary at that new Thai restaurant." No one likes a guilt-tripper or scorekeeper. The same applies to adult children. If you want them to call or text more often, don't say, "I never hear from you." Say, "Good to hear from you," when they do call. Assume they are busy, and don't text, ask them lots of questions, or tell them what to do.

Day 300: He Means Well

SATURDAY

You tell your husband that you're overwhelmed by all the things you have to do and "need a break." He says, "A break from what?" So you explain that besides work, you have to deal with daycare, playdates, and your parents, as well as exercise, clean, and do errands. He still doesn't see what's so hard. That's because he's a man and most men like to solve problems, not complain or explain. The problem is you're expecting sympathy from a man. If you called a woman and told her your to-do list and that you needed a break, she would say, "Of course." So tell your girlfriends!

Day 301: Be an Efficiency Expert

SUNDAY

A client called to say that she and her husband had a fight and wanted to know how she could have handled it better. They both work full-time while raising ten-year-old twins, yet he expects her to make all the restaurant reservations and book vacations, in addition to planning playdates and handling the holidays. She told him, "Why don't you call the restaurant? I have a million things to do today." They bickered for ten minutes about who does more. We said, "In the time you argued, you could have made reservations. Don't be right, be efficient!

Apply *The Rules* to Achieve Your Higher Self

1   Don't think that fighting is normal or that all couples fight. Actor
    George Clooney claims that he and his human rights lawyer wife
    Amal have never had a fight. Let them be your role model for
    marriage. Don't assume it's because they're millionaires. Many
    wealthy couples fight and divorce. No, we believe it's because
    they are both philanthropists. When your mind is on important
    issues with your *Higher Self*, you have no time to quarrel or be
    petty *Lower Self*!

2   When your husband drives you crazy with his OCD or daily
    mishigas, remind yourself that he is doing it, not doing it to you!
    Your husband is not trying to annoy you—he just happens to be
    annoying. It's not personal, which should take the sting out of it
    and help you not react and go about your business unaffected.

3   If you grew up with screamers or yell when you argue, take a
    deep breath, pause, and try to talk softly or even whisper. Your
    husband will tune you out if you scream, but his ears will perk up
    if you whisper, as it's both refreshing and feminine. Your soft-
    spoken message will be heard more clearly than shouting it.

WEEK SIX

Choose Forgiveness over Fighting

Your *Rules* Weekly Pep Talk

When you empower your *Higher Self* and choose forgiveness over fighting, your marriage will be much happier and your husband will feel more connected to you. Marriage will hopefully bring out the best in you (love and kindness), but sometimes it will bring out the worst in you (hate and selfishness).

This week, no matter how upset you are with your husband, allow your *Higher Self* to guide you in your thoughts of forgiveness, compassion, and seeking to understand. Don't give into your *Lower Self* where the world revolves around you, he doesn't understand you, and you want what you want and don't care about what he wants. Take the high ground unless it's a deal-breaker like cheating or financial fraud. Give him a pass, and then let it go.

CHOOSE FORGIVING, OVER FIGHTING
Daily *Rules*

Day 302: Don't Fight
MONDAY

Today the divorce rate is at 50%, and there are many reasons why. One cause is that when a woman chooses to fight from her *Lower Self*, because she doesn't like something about her husband, she often complains to him and also finds three girlfriends to take her side. They might say, "OMG, I would never put up with that," or "Maybe you should have stayed with your ex who made more money." So she fights with her husband, stops speaking to him, withholds intimacy, lives her own life (dinners and trips to spas with those girlfriends), thinks the grass is greener (envying her friends' husbands), acts single, and forgets her vows.

Day 303: Give Him a Pass
TUESDAY

Let's say your husband doesn't call you to say he's running late for dinner, forgets to pick up the dry cleaning on the way home, or takes a call from his friend in the middle of your date night. Don't blow up (*Lower Self*). You wouldn't blow up if your best friend was running late or took a personal call. Pretend he's a coworker and give him a pass (*Higher Self*) because (a) he's your life partner and (b) you never know when you're going to make a mistake and need his mercy and forgiveness.

Day 304: Lower Your Expectations
WEDNESDAY

Stop expecting your husband to show you love exactly the way you want him to. "If he loved me, he would..." is the national anthem for many married women. A client called because she was angry her husband wasn't doing anything special for her birthday, which reminded her of how her parents did little for her. She decided to celebrate with a group of girlfriends instead. We said don't do it. What would you like him to do? She said a fancy dinner alone or with friends would be nice. We advised her to tell him what she would prefer, and he went all out. She wrote to us, "Thank you. You saved my birthday. It was a perfect day." Her *Lower Self* wanted to sabotage her birthday and have a pity party, but with some coaching, her *Higher Self* prevailed.

Day 305: Don't Poke the Bear
THURSDAY

Not speaking to men first doesn't just apply to dating. When you're married and your husband isn't in the mood to talk, give him some space. You might think this is crazy because he's your husband, but if you sense he would rather read the newspaper or is stressed about work or just wants to be alone in his recliner in his man cave, talk to someone else and don't poke the bear. If you speak to him when he's in a bad mood, you run the risk of getting hurt by snippy remarks, such as, "How would I know?" "Why would you ask me that?" or "I can't talk now!" Ouch! It is better to wait and say, "I'd like to share something with you. When's a good time?"

Day 306: Sorry Not Sorry
FRIDAY

Women get upset when their husbands don't apologize. They tell us, "I'm not talking to him until he says he's sorry for getting drunk at my friend's wedding," or "He yelled at me for no reason. I want an apology." Most men don't like to admit when they're wrong and just like to move on after a disagreement as if nothing happened, so don't hold your breath. It's nice if you get an apology, but don't sleep in another room if you don't. The best way to change someone is by example, so apologize the next time you make a mistake and show him the right way by example.

Day 307: Never Use the D Word
SATURDAY

Sometimes a married client will call with an emergency consultation. Her husband wants a divorce. Invariably we find out that she used the D word many times before, and now he's reacting in kind and mirroring what she said. Throwing around the D word in a fight is poisonous. If you don't really want a divorce, don't say the D word or anything like it, such as "I wish I never married you." Remember, we said not to use the M word (marriage) when dating, ditto for the D word now. Whether you're using it for shock value or to hurt your husband, it always backfires. *Higher Self* chooses words carefully to keep the peace, while *Lower Self* loves to sow seeds of discourse. Maybe the divorce rate is 50% because the D word was tossed around too many times.

Day 308: Remember Why You Love Him
SUNDAY

Some married women have amnesia. They forget why they fell in love with their partners and only focus on his faults from their *Lower Self,* such as he's grumpy, he snores, he is glued to sports and video games, or he talks too much or too little. Of course, it doesn't come naturally to remember the moment you decided he was The One and couldn't wait for his next call, text, or date. Just like you don't walk around all day thinking, "Thank God, I have two arms and two legs." You don't always think about how lucky you are to be married. You take your husband for granted. To be happily married, remember how much you wanted to marry him. *Higher Self!*

Apply *The Rules* to Achieve Your Higher Self

1   If an argument is escalating and it's getting late, don't force yourself to resolve it that night. Go to bed. Everything is better in the morning.

2   Don't demand an apology. If he doesn't say he's sorry or it's not from his heart, it won't mean anything anyway. It's more important that he changes or you accept him as he is than he apologizes.

3   Don't fight about silly things, like who forgot to change the toilet paper. If you see something that needs to be done, just do it.

WEEK SEVEN
You Have All the Power to Create a Happy Marriage

Your *Rules* Weekly Pep Talk

We can't change other people—we can only change ourselves. So, when you go into marriage, don't expect the other partner to change. Accept them as they are, unless their actions or behaviors are destructive or violent.

A *Rules* marriage is happy because you are a team player. Change yourself, follow the family leader, and don't fight against human nature. Work together and support him as a valuable member of your family team. When you support your husband and respect his masculine side, he will be thrilled. And when you embrace your feminine side, you will be diplomatic, not bossy, and you won't insist on always getting your way or being right.

This week, focus on helping and cheerleading your husband, not harassing him. You're on his side because his side is your side. This week, focus on being on Team _____ (your family's last name)!

YOU HAVE THE POWER TO CREATE A HAPPY MARRIAGE
Daily *Rules*

Day 309: The Power of Taking the High Ground
MONDAY

You might think that *The Rules for Marriage* are one-sided. You're the one being easy to be with, you're letting him win, and you're not complaining or saying the D word. Why are you supposed to try acting like a saint? What's in it for you? A lot! You get security and devotion, cards and flowers for no occasion, a guy who opens doors and holds up the umbrella in the rain, and a husband who wants to grow old with you. We know women whose husbands forget Valentine's Day or their wedding anniversary. These women are probably not doing *The Rules for Marriage*, so they get that kind of husband and not your husband!

Day 310: Choose Empathy
TUESDAY

You mention that you're tired. Your husband again says, "Tired from what?" Your girlfriends would probably say, "I'm sure you do so much." Don't blow up at him for being insensitive. Just say "Oh, this and that." He doesn't mean anything by it. Most men are just not wired to be sympathetic. He thinks he's being rational by asking. Don't tell him, "You have zero empathy." Men are not raised to call each other if they have a cold or back pain. Women, on the other hand, will text three friends that they got their period or didn't sleep well. Women bond over sharing their problems ("These cramps are unbelievable!"), while men bond over competition and success ("The Yankees won!") If you can't accept his reaction, don't tell him you're tired. Tell your girlfriends!

Day 311: Avoid Telling Him What to Do
WEDNESDAY

Don't tell your husband what to do. Yes, you read that right—pretend you're dating him again and don't let your domineering *Lower Self* come out and try to force your will on him. When you need his help with something, let him know how important it is to you first. You cannot make him make more money or lose weight or stop drinking or smoking or pick up his clothes off the floor or whatever he's doing or not doing. You can't make him work less if he's a workaholic. You can't make him work more if he's not ambitious. He's not five years old. Stay in your own lane. Live your own life. The only deal-breakers are betrayal, infidelity, and stealing your money, but if you absolutely must have your way with an issue—for example you want a new living room set—say "This is important to me. Maybe it can be an anniversary present?"

Day 312: Complaining Is Ineffective
THURSDAY

You think your husband drinks or eats too much. He's a slob. He's addicted to sports. He takes forever to get to the point

when you ask him a question. Whatever it is, you wish he
was more self-aware like you! When you were dating, you
barely noticed his bad habits because you were so in love and
wanted to marry him. Maybe you secretly thought you could
change him. Now you're investing your energy to constantly
fix him from your *Lower Self.* Ask your *Higher Self* what you
would be doing if you weren't focused on him. Why not be
productive instead of nagging him about his bad habits or
things you don't like? Be careful. Realize he can easily turn
around and do the same to you.

Day 313: Accepting Correction

FRIDAY

Most husbands tend to be efficiency experts. Yours may
notice that you hate to cook and love to shop. You don't
want him to tell you what to do. But if you think *Higher Self*
thoughts, that your husband was put in your life to help you
become the best version of yourself, you will take correction.
Women who love to order take-out food are now whipping
up dishes because their husbands wanted more home-
cooked meals. Other women are getting out of debt because
their husbands put a stop to their out-of-control shopping
for designer bags and shoes. Instead of getting annoyed or
arguing, try to think of your husband as your biggest helper!

Day 314: Don't Try to Change Him
SATURDAY

As we keep mentioning, women often marry a man thinking that they will change him. They quickly realize they can't and shouldn't. If he's a workaholic, don't ask him to be home for dinner at 6 pm, play boardgames, or do puzzles every night. Only help him change if he asks for help. Besides, the best way to change him for the better is by example. If he sees you modeling your *Higher Self* (eating right, exercising, and being positive, happy, and busy), instead of your *Lower Self* (being lazy, annoyed, or complaining), he will be more attracted to you and want to be a better man for you.

Day 315: Stay Out of Results
SUNDAY

Don't follow up to see if your husband or anyone in your life is using your advice, as curious as you may be. They should contact you, much like a guy has to call to ask you out for the next date. Showing too much interest in the outcome is controlling and desperate. You are happy and busy with your own life, not consumed with theirs. You are humble and helpful, not ego-driven or playing savior or looking to be thanked. You're not codependent and so focused on solving other people's problems that you ignore your own. Spiritual teacher Emmet Fox said, "Those who mind other people's business neglect their own."

Apply *The Rules* to Achieve Your Higher Self

1   Your instinct may be to react or fight when your husband inadvertently triggers you. So pause and think how best to "not step into the pothole," whether that means running into another room, calling a friend later to calm down, or tabling the conversation for twenty-four hours. You have choices, so don't act like a victim.

2   If your husband says your credit card bill has never been higher and it's all your fault (holiday shopping and too many spa days with your girlfriends), don't get defensive or scream, "Maybe it's those fancy golf clubs and season tickets to the Knicks that put us in debt!" Calmly look at the statement and see where the money went, show him the facts and figures, and vow to do better. Don't retaliate when he overreacts!

3   *Rules for Marriage* 101. In any argument, stick to the topic. Don't throw in the kitchen sink and say, "And another thing, remember when you . . . " A man can only take so much!

WEEK EIGHT
Marriage Is a Balancing Act

Your *Rules* Weekly Pep Talk

Some people think that life before marriage is overwhelming. Then, once they get married and have a family, life can seem like walking on a tightrope. There is so much competition for a married woman's attention today, whether it's her big career, her home renovations, girls' night out, kickboxing class, social media, and sometimes kids.

Be sure you don't spread yourself so thin that you have nothing left to give your husband. Don't be so busy that you forget to cook dinner (his favorite meal) and give him cold leftovers or neglect to be playful or intimate. You need to still date him, even when you're married. If you're too busy to be a wife, then you're too busy. Drop some of the other activities and act like you're dating your husband again. Spend more time nurturing your relationship and intimacy to strengthen your marriage.

This week, focus on getting your priorities straight—your husband first and everything else after. Send him flirty texts, thank him for all the small things he does for you and your family, and tell him how attractive and sexy he is.

MARRIAGE IS A BALANCING ACT
Daily *Rules*

Day 316: Marriage Before Career
MONDAY

It's difficult for high-powered women to remember that their marriages are more important than their careers. One client complained her husband asked her to pick up dinner on her way home from work. She complained, "As if I have nothing better to do. Why can't he get it?" Another client said, "Why doesn't he put the dishes in the dishwasher? It's not like his arms are broken!" We said sometimes you have to act like catering to your husband's needs, cooking, and housework are more important than your work (*wink, wink*)! If your husband and home life isn't happy, it doesn't matter what you do for a living.

Day 317: Don't Expect Applause
TUESDAY

Even in this age of dual-career couples, most of the housework and kids' work falls on the wife or mother, and your husband probably doesn't thank you for each and every task. You want to scream, "Do you think this house looks this way by magic? Who do you think makes the beds? Mary Poppins?" Your husband thinks he said thank you once and that should last for twenty years. Similarly, you don't thank him every time he takes out the garbage. Don't be a score-keeper as your *Lower Self*. A marriage is like any other relationship: You do things, he does other things, it all evens out in the *Higher Self's* opinion in the end, and a happy marriage is your thank you!

Day 318: Time-Saver
WEDNESDAY

It annoys your husband that you're always on your phone. He says something sarcastic like "I'm used to it." Don't say, "Well, I'm used to you watching sports!" Your *Lower Self* loves a good fight, but your *Higher Self* could have avoided it by saying, "You're right, I really should do a phone detox" and put away the cell phone. You would never tell a good friend that you "put up with" anything. You'll save lots of time by getting along with your husband. Think of all the calls to girlfriends and your therapist you won't have to make saying, "He's sleeping on the couch" or "We're not talking!"

Day 319: Nice at Home
THURSDAY

Sometimes it's easier to be nicer to your children, friends, coworkers, and boss than your husband. They don't snore, notice your faults, act bossy, talk loudly, accidentally put your new fishnet bathing suit in the dryer, or are just annoying! Sometimes it is so much easier to be nicer to a stranger than your husband! If a friend or acquaintance said she wanted to start a new business, you would say, "You go girl," but if your husband suggests it, you say, "Oh yeah, like your last project and with what money?" Don't make him your punching bag!

Day 320: Make Time for Intimacy

FRIDAY

Don't think, what's the least I can do and still stay married?
Women, especially working moms, want to cut corners by
saying no to intimacy or cooking because they are tired
or have an early morning Pilates class or their evening
book club. This is a mistake. Intimacy and cooking are to
men what snuggling is to women. One benefit of a *Rules*
marriage is that your husband finds you attractive and
loves your cooking, so be flattered. Try to put yourself in
the mood because it's not about feeling it all the time, but
doing it. Physical intimacy leads to emotional intimacy.
Everyone wins!

Day 321: Unified Front

SATURDAY

A big mistake married women make is putting their children
before their husbands. They may side with their kids when
their husband is trying to discipline them and treat him like
the Big Bad Wolf. Back each other up and be a unified front
so your kids don't divide and conquer. They are probably
already entitled and not as innocent as you think! Also,
be honest: Are you trying to get your kids' love by giving
them what they want (more stuff) instead of what they need
(discipline)? Are you trying to be their favorite parent? When
they move out, it will be you and your husband, so get your
priorities straight and be on the same page now!

Day 322: Accept Your Partner for Who He Is
SUNDAY

People who try to get their partners to change one thing inevitably pick on something else soon after. For example, a client was upset about her husband's drinking, so he attended Alcoholics Anonymous and quit alcohol. She was happy for about a month that he was sober but then was annoyed that he was going to a meeting every night, leaving her alone for an hour or two. With our coaching, she realized it was always going to be something that bothered her and got busy with her own life. At our suggestion, she joined Al-Anon, a support group for the friends and family of alcoholics, and met other women in the same predicament. They met for coffee and worked on their own issues. She learned she was codependent and that she had character defects (anger, expectations, and moodiness), just like her husband, that needed to be corrected to be happily married. Her entire world opened up, and her attitude changed from self-pity and sadness to acceptance and gratitude. Her *Lower Self* wanted to be mad and sulk about her situation, but her *Higher Self* sought spirituality and happiness. Sometimes being annoyed with your spouse is not about your spouse at all, but misdirected anger. What are you really upset about? Dig deep! Figure that out first and you will be more content and less angry at your partner.

Apply *The Rules* to Achieve Your Higher Self

1   When a girlfriend calls to make plans, don't forget to check with your husband first, out of respect and courtesy and just in case there's a conflict.

2   When you want to put your children before your husband, remember that you're not only disrespecting your husband, but spoiling your children.

3   Don't copy other women who complain about their husbands or put them last. If everyone jumped out of a window, would you?

WEEK NINE

Don't Betray Your Marriage

Your *Rules* Weekly Pep Talk

Have you ever been hurt or betrayed? It doesn't feel good and can destroy loving and long-lasting relationships. If you want to be happily married, try to remember that you are your husband's wife before you're a mother, daughter, sister, friend, coworker, or head honcho of XYZ company. Your time and devotion should be to your husband first.

When you grasp this concept, your relationship with your partner will fall into place. Without healthy and loving actions and intentions between husband and wife, there is no caring and stable family, so follow *The Rules for Marriage* and nurture your marriage first. Never betray your marriage by choosing someone else over him, talking behind his back, or making him look bad in front of others.

This week, focus on aligning your allegiance and identity with your husband first and let everyone and everything else follow.

DON'T BETRAY YOUR MARRIAGE
Daily *Rules*

Day 323: Mind Your Own Business
MONDAY

Some people are convinced they must tell their spouse, friend, or family member that they have a problem. "If I notice something about someone, that they're drinking or eating too much or isolating, I feel obligated to say something, whether or not they ask. What kind of person ignores a problem?" While this sounds good in theory, it rarely changes their behavior. People change when they are in enough pain or are motivated to do so, not because someone points it out. A mother was concerned about her twenty-five-year-old son's weight. We told her to stay out of it. He fell in love with a girl, got a trainer, and lost the weight on his own.

Day 324: On the Down-Low
TUESDAY

If you have a best friend, older sister, or mother who is overly influential in your life, try not to mention her name too much to your husband. You don't want him thinking that you and your friend or relative are running your life and he's just a stuffed shirt or cardboard figure. Your husband could feel emasculated if he thinks "Lucy and Ethel" are deciding on whether you should use a nanny or daycare or where to go on vacation. He wants to think that you are a team, and it's you and him against the world. If you mention her name too often, he may get the feeling that you're really married to her, not him!

Day 325: Don't Forget to Be Nice to Your Husband
WEDNESDAY

Are you nice to everyone but your husband? We know many women who are wonderful mothers, daughters, friends, workers, bosses, and clients, but are not so nice and even downright rude to their husbands. How can you be a lovely person with everyone in your life but not with your husband? Because it's easy to be polite to people you don't live with. Your husband can be a lot of work or bossy. All he talks about is food (what's for dinner?) or aluminum siding (yawn!) or being intimate (again?) or saving money (no more stilettos). Your *Lower Self* might say," What about my needs?" But what you don't realize is meeting his needs inspires him to meet your needs in return. You may have also thought, "Yippee, I did *The Rules*, I got him, and now I can relax!" You actually still need to take actions to nurture your relationship with him and his needs. When you show you care about him by being a good listener, sticking to a budget, preparing meals, and being intimate, you will have a happier marriage.

Day 326: First or Last?
THURSDAY

Are you putting your work, friends, parents, money, social status or social media, fantasies about what your husband

or marriage should be like, your feelings, or all of the above
before your husband? Is your husband first in your life,
somewhere in the middle, or last? Do you even think about
him that much anymore? You have so much going on! You
have plenty of time and energy for your friends, your kids,
the gym, and hobbies but are bored and tired when your
husband wants something. You find him annoying. He leaves
shaving cream on the counter or underwear on the floor. You
fantasize about a pristine house with him not in it. Stop these
Lower Self thoughts or you'll be single in a perfectly clean
house! Honoring your husband is *Higher Self.*

Day 327: Stop Acting Single

FRIDAY

You're married, but consult everyone else: your therapist,
sister, friends, decorator, trainer, stylist, and psychic for
advice before him or instead of him. You order furniture
based on your decorator. You decide about your health or
finances based on your astrologer instead of discussing it with
your husband. No wonder he feels left out. Don't think "I
put myself through college. I don't have to ask his permission
about how to spend money." This is your *Lower Self* talking.
You took vows. You have to be respectful (*Higher Self*). Ask his
advice and his permission, even if it's about having a girls'
night out or ordering drapes. If you keep acting single, you
will be single!

Day 328: Don't Bad-Mouth Your Partner

SATURDAY

When did women become so sarcastic and not soft and loving? Many women talk and act like badasses, as if they have a cigar in their mouths. It's fine for work but terrible for marriage. They love to be cynical and clever at their husband's expense. They're like female stand-up comedians. Women love to bash their husbands and gravitate to other women who do the same. Misery loves company. Don't be the partner who talks badly about her husband! It's not charming and reflects poorly on you (*Lower Self*). Your friends and relatives might permanently remember these criticisms and think less of your husband. *Higher Self* finds the good in everyone, especially your husband!

Day 329: A Mansion without a Man

SUNDAY

A married client got the renovation bug and put her dream home before her husband. She was so busy breaking down walls and picking out kitchen countertops that she was too busy to cook and keep their home running smoothly. Her husband said they couldn't afford it, but she wouldn't stop. He filed for a separation. At first, she was shocked. How could an innocent home renovation create so much havoc? But we explained that she completely bulldozed him. We told her to apologize and tell him she would rather live in a cardboard box with him than a mansion without him. She stopped renovating and spending. He came back!

Apply *The Rules* to Achieve Your Higher Self

1 When a family member or friend suggests an idea that your husband is against, side with your husband, even if it means disappointing or even losing that friend.

2 When you're eating dinner with your husband and he wants to talk, get off your phone. Be respectful and just be with him.

3 Even if you don't think your husband has all the answers, ask him for advice and include him in decisions, as you do your therapist or girlfriends, so you're not two ships passing in the night.

WEEK TEN

Betrayal, Cheating, & Divorce

Your *Rules* Weekly Pep Talk

You got married thinking it was forever, but it's no longer looking that way. He cheated and wants to be with her now, not you, or he cheated and wants you back, but you can't trust him anymore. Or maybe you just don't get along but he refuses to go to counseling, or his bad habits like drinking or drugging or raging are too much for you to handle. These are all marriage challenges that are difficult to deal with, but with help, you might be able to persevere. If he betrayed you by gambling or using drugs or won't get help for his alcoholism, it's time to set firm boundaries by your *Higher Self* or take a break.

If he's having an affair, we feel it's over and time to get a divorce. We're all for forgiveness, but we draw the line at cheating. We believe that cheating is a deal-breaker and once a cheater, always a cheater.

Focus this week on what you can do to change yourself, advocate for him to get help from an expert, and stay in your power so you can better navigate the ups and downs of betrayal or cheating and make the best decision for both partners.

BETRAYAL, CHEATING, & DIVORCE
Daily *Rules*

Day 330: No Magic Pill

Some women think that marriage counseling is a magic pill that will make their husbands change for the better. They want to talk about everything, and their husbands usually don't. We hate to burst their bubble, but counseling will only help if it's his idea to go. If it's not his idea, he will refuse, agree and then cancel, or fight with you before, during, and after the session, and it will be another thing you fight about. He even might feel that you and the counselor are ganging up on him. The magic pill for marriage is being loving, using your *Higher Self*, and not complaining or changing him (*Lower Self*).

Day 331: Don't Romanticize Being Single

When your husband is driving you crazy, it's easy to romanticize being single. When you were single, you could do whatever you felt like, talk to your girlfriends all night, put your hair in a messy bun and not wear a bra or makeup, get takeout and cook less and organize more, and turn the heat up (you're always cold). Thinking that being single was fun is *Lower Self*. Your *Higher Self* remembers bad dates, lonely Saturday nights and holidays, no one to hold hands with at the movies, and looking at Facebook posts of happy couples and is grateful to be married!

Day 332: One Cheat and It's Over
WEDNESDAY

We're all for forgiveness, but we draw the line at cheating. We believe that cheating is a deal-breaker and once a cheater, possibly always a cheater. *The Rules* apply to both partners. If your husband had or is having a sexual relationship with another woman, your marriage is most likely over. How can you trust him? That's the problem, you can't. If you decide to "stand by your man," your marriage will never be the same and you might feel insecure, constantly check his phone, and wonder what he's doing when he's not home. *The Rules* are about feeling secure, not anxiety-ridden and shaking! However, there are rare exceptions where it was a one-time affair and he's beyond devastated and remorseful, will do anything to win you back, and does it.

Day 333: Looking the Other Way
THURSDAY

Women who find out after they're exclusive or married that the guy is cheating or bad with money admit that they saw red flags and looked the other way. They remember he skipped Saturday nights without explanation when they were dating, but they pretended not to care. They noticed that he always seemed to forget his wallet and asked them to pay or suggested get-rich-quick schemes, but they didn't think it was a big deal, only to find out he was in serious debt. If you ignored red flags or pink flags, don't be surprised if these behaviors resurface.

Day 334: Live and Let Live

FRIDAY

Your husband's cheating is grounds for divorce, but his watching porn or X-rated movies is not. This does not include talking or having online chats, because that would be considered cheating. We understand his porn addiction may make you feel not good enough or pretty enough, but that's your *Lower Self* talking. No one can make you feel good enough or not good enough but you. As long as he is initiating intimacy, doesn't have an online girlfriend, and isn't asking you to do anything uncomfortable, let it go. The more you focus on this bad habit, the more he will want to do it or do it in secret. He probably finds your bad habits equally annoying.

Day 335: Stop Resisting and Move On

SATURDAY

Unfortunately, marriages don't always last. Sometimes it's because the beginning wasn't right (you chased him or got pregnant and that's why he proposed), you didn't do *The Rules for Marriage* (you were hard to be with), or you grew apart. Whatever the reason, divorce can be devastating for women ("I'll never meet anyone, I'm older, men want women half my age..."). If your husband wants out no matter what you say or do, you need to move on. Your *Lower Self* wants the status quo at any cost ("Just tell me how to get him back"), but your *Higher Self* knows it's never going to work and that the Universe has better plans!

Day 336: Divorce with Dignity

SUNDAY

Other reasons to end a marriage: alcoholism and drug abuse (unless he's willing to go to rehab or Alcoholics Anonymous), rage and physical violence, and stealing your money (maybe he's a compulsive gambler who bet away your home). Other reasons are less tangible: You've grown apart, you've met someone else, or one of you has fallen out of love. We don't believe in staying in an abusive or loveless marriage. If you decide to end it, take the high road. Don't play the blame game or bad-mouth him. Your *Lower Self* might want to destroy him, but your *Higher Self* divorces with dignity.

Apply *The Rules* to Achieve Your Higher Self

1 Don't assume marriage counseling is the answer. No matter what your husband does or doesn't do, you still have to work on yourself, your attitude, your anger, and your expectations.

2 Before you call a divorce lawyer, think about the cons of splitting up, like legal fees, custody, and dating again!

3 Before you file, remember why you married him and how you hated being single!

WEEK ELEVEN
Regrets & Reevaluation

Your *Rules* Weekly Pep Talk

Do you have regrets about your past love life? Who doesn't? Some single women call us to talk about an ex from five or even ten years ago who they can't stop thinking about! If only they had done this or that, they would be married to him! But if he was so great or The One, why aren't they married to him now?

We quickly realize during our conversations with the client that she didn't use *The Rules* and made the first move, or he disappeared after three months or wouldn't commit after five years. We advise them to stop fantasizing about the past and focus their energy on meeting someone else. We remind them that if they insist on holding onto some past fantasy guy, they will certainly regret wasting more time.

Focus this week on asking yourself, "Am I living my best life now, or am I creating more future regrets?"

Daily *Rules*

Day 337: The Power of Now
MONDAY

There are many theories about how long it should take to heal from a breakup. Some say to wait a month for every year you were married, so if you were married for twelve years, you should wait a year! We respectfully disagree! We believe you should start dating immediately. Do you wait months or years to look for work after being fired from a job? We don't think so. We tell clients to post their profile on dating apps and go to a speed-dating event that night or ASAP. Too many smart and successful women are still "recovering" from men they dated five years ago! We tell them to stop waiting and start dating now!

Day 338: Don't Pick on Yourself
TUESDAY

The first thing a woman does after a divorce or breakup is pick on herself! She's convinced she's a failure and that no one is going to want her. She is talkative (or too quiet), independent (or codependent), damaged goods, never been in a good relationship, can't put cool outfits together . . . you get the picture! We tell her, "No, no, the guy who loves you will love your quirkiness, and he'll want whatever you are. When they love you, they don't see anything wrong with you."

Day 339: Regrets

WEDNESDAY

When you were married and your husband was annoying, you couldn't think of anything good about him! Maybe you should have made a gratitude list: He asked you to marry him, took out the garbage, paid the bills, planned interesting vacations, made you laugh, never forgot your birthday or wedding anniversary or Valentine's Day, read you the news so you didn't have to, taped your favorite TV shows because you aren't good with the DVR, put up with your PMS and moodiness, shoveled the snow at 5 am, gave you back rubs, and opened your packages so you didn't break a nail. Reflect on his acts of kindness and think about getting back together, if that's an option.

Day 340: One Call for Closure

THURSDAY

You might be thinking, "If I had only done *The Rules* on my ex-boyfriend, we might still be together. Can I get him back?" It depends! If you initiated the relationship, spoke to him first, asked him out, and he eventually ended it, there is no hope and it was never meant to be. But if he pursued you, you became clingy, and he felt suffocated and broke it off, there may be a chance. There's only one way to find out, and we call it "one call or text for closure." Call or text and say, "Hi, I was just wondering how you are doing..." If he doesn't call, text back, or ask to meet, it's over!

Day 341: Moving On

When women contact us for help, they usually want to talk about their exes. We encourage them to stop talking about them and go on dating apps and singles events ASAP because the best way to get over an ex is to meet someone else. We tell them to wipe away a tear, post photos and a light and breezy profile, and wait for men to contact them. There's nothing like getting messages ("Hey beautiful") to help you get over your ex. Your *Lower Self* wants to live in the past and is all about lack, comfort, and limitation. Your *Higher Self* is all about the future, new possibilities, and abundance.

Day 342: Decluttering Your Ex

Getting over your ex is a lot like decluttering your closet. During makeover consultations, we tell clients what to get rid of. Some argue, "I can't. This is my favorite top." We say, "No, it's not flattering. No one is wearing that color. It's a turtleneck. It's not good for dating. Give it to Goodwill." The clients who argue don't succeed as fast as the clients who readily agree with our suggestions. The compliant clients are too busy buying the right clothes instead of crying about the frumpy ones. It's the same with exes. The faster you let go of your ex, the sooner you'll meet Mr. Right.

Day 343: Don't Stay Stuck

SUNDAY

Are you struggling with the end of your marriage or a breakup? Are you frustrated that he has moved on so quickly and you haven't? You're not alone! Unfortunately, men can end a five-year relationship in five minutes and meet someone new that night, while women tend to stay stuck and suffer! Maybe it wasn't even a relationship but an online fantasy guy who bombarded you with texts and then disappeared. Force yourself to believe that the breakup is for a reason and that the Universe has a better plan and a better man for you, even if you can't see it now. Move on!

Apply *The Rules* to Achieve Your Higher Self

1   If you broke up with your ex and then realized he is a good guy after all and the problem was you not appreciating him or thinking the grass is greener, take him back! It's easier than starting all over again!

2   After a breakup or divorce, there's nothing to be gained by waiting to date. You're not going to be any wiser, you already know *The Rules*, and you're only going to be older!

3   Don't pick on yourself or think that you are not ready or not good enough to date now. Tell yourself you are perfect just the way you are while you are getting dressed to go out to meet men, whether or not you believe it or feel it. You don't have to feel ready or pretty to date!

WEEK TWELVE

Starting Over with *The Rules*

Your *Rules* Weekly Pep Talk

No one wants to break up or get a divorce and then start over. Everyone intrinsically likes stability and prefers the status quo. But if you're single, separated, or divorced, you don't have a choice. You either go out and join dating apps or you live your life alone. For some women, that is fine, but most of our readers prefer to be in a committed relationship.

So what do you do now that you're single? We recommend you begin your dating journey by reading and using *The Rules* all over again. If you were successful at finding your marriage partner the first time, you will do it again and will be even wiser the second time around.

This week, focus on getting out of your comfort zone, showing up for dates, practicing *The Rules*, and finding support with a *Rules* dating coach, *Rules* Facebook group, therapist, or *Rules*-minded girlfriends.

Daily *Rules*

Day 344: Dating after Divorce
MONDAY

Divorced women who have been through the wringer are
often reluctant to date again. They are nervous about not
being good enough or young enough or pretty enough. They
fear they will never meet anyone who wants them because of
their age and baggage. They worry about finding a babysit-
ter even though they don't even have a date! We tell them
these are all limiting *Lower Self* thoughts. *Higher Self* is all
about moving on and having hope. We tell them to post their
profile and photos on dating apps and find singles events in
their area. The best way to get over an ex is to meet someone better!

Day 345: Don't Be Naïve
TUESDAY

If you've been married and out of the dating scene for years
or decades, you might believe that it's different now, that a
woman can make the first move. Of course, a woman can
do anything she wants, but will it work? We don't think so!
Anyone who tells you that you can pursue a man successfully
is telling you what you want to hear. Don't be gullible. It's
like telling you that you can eat all you want without gaining
weight. It's a scam. If it sounds too good to be true, it is. So
don't believe in any dating app or philosophy that tells you to

message men first. It's a fantasy. You're going to waste time or get hurt!

Day 346: Date ASAP

WEDNESDAY

Some suggest wellness retreats in India and detoxing from men after a divorce. We suggest just the opposite. Jump into the dating pool ASAP or you will forget how to date and it will become harder later on. If you wait, you will become like all your other divorced friends who have not met anyone in ten years because they're so busy with divorce support groups and fighting with their ex. Nothing can replace dressing up and dating. Of course, give yourself five minutes a day to break down, look at your wedding album, and cry, but then get glammed up and go out to singles events and post your profile!

Day 347: Clean Break

THURSDAY

It used to be that when a couple broke up; it was over and done with. No contact! Now we have messy on-and-off-again breakups because women refuse to let go and move on. Typically, a guy will break up with a woman but say he would be open to being friends. A Rules Girl would find this completely unacceptable, a demotion, and an insult. She doesn't want a friend; she wants a boyfriend and future husband. A non-Rules Girl will continue to see him (she bought show tickets for his birthday before they broke up, or it's New Year's Eve and they spent the last five years celebrating it and she can't imagine watching the ball drop with anyone else) and sometimes also sleep with him. This is a complete waste of time, as it will give you false hope and possibly keep you from dating others. There is no dignity in seeing an ex for any reason or being friends with or without benefits unless you have children. For the sake of the kids, you should be friendly, but you should not be friends.

Day 348: Rebound Girl
FRIDAY

While you should never date a married man, you can date a man who is separated as long as he is not living with his wife. You don't have to wait until he is 100% divorced, but don't be his rebound girl. A rebound girl is the girl he wastes time with to get over his ex. If his ex left him and he's still hung up on her, run. If he left her and only talks to her about their children, you have nothing to worry about. But if he says he never wants to get married again and treats you like his therapist to vent about fights with his ex and custody battles, you need to know nothing more. Move on.

Day 349: Recently Separated
SATURDAY

If a recently separated guy is constantly talking about his ex, he probably doesn't like you. When a guy likes you, he only wants to talk about you! He seems like he's in a trance, he can't stop looking at you, he can barely look at the menu, and

he can't believe he met you! He wants to know everything
about you: your childhood, your career, your hobbies, and
your favorite books, TV shows, movies, and music. He'll ask
about your family and friends. He'll talk about concerts and
shows he wants to take you to. If he's talking about his ex,
he's either still in love with her or using you as a therapist.

Day 350: Reminder

FRIDAY

When we say don't talk or text a man first, some women
argue, "There's nothing wrong with starting a conversation.
You can always text him to see if he is available to connect.
If he asks you out, great. If not, you have nothing to lose."
Wrong! You do have something to lose: time! When you
initiate a relationship, it usually doesn't work out long term.
He will eventually feel that something isn't right or something
is missing for him. A year or more later, he will end it and
maybe not even know why, but we will. It's because you
made the first move! Rules Girls don't waste time!

Day 351: Before You Jump into Dating

SUNDAY

Dating after a breakup or divorce can be scary, but you don't
have to do it alone. You can join *Rules* Facebook support
groups. You can attend twelve-step support groups such
as Alcoholics Anonymous if you are drinking because of
your dating, Overeaters Anonymous if you are overeating
because of your emotions, Sex and Love Addicts Anonymous

if you are addicted to love and need better boundaries, Misery Addicts Anonymous if you are self-sabotaging your relationships, and Recovery Inc. for mental-health issues such as anxiety, anger, and fear. Get support in between dates so you're never alone.

Apply *The Rules* to Achieve Your Higher Self

1   If you're dating after a breakup or divorce, you may think that everything is different now, with dating apps and social media. It's not! Technology has changed the way people meet, but the guy still has to make the first move in whatever medium and you still have to play hard to get!

2   If a guy talks about his ex a lot, Buyer Beware. He's not over her or not that into you! Don't waste time and move on!

3   Doing nothing is not an option if you're single, separated, or divorced. You need to go out and join dating apps and try something, anything, one thing! Break the ice!

COURSE 6

The Rules
Refresher
Course

2 WEEKS

For the last twenty-five-plus years, we've helped thousands of women around the world use *The Rules* to meet and marry their lifelong partners and hope you have created many healthy and long-lasting relationships after reading and using the Weekly Pep Talks and Daily Lessons in this book!

If you relate to this book, there may have been times when you were hurt, discouraged, or disappointed while looking for a healthy relationship with the right lifelong partner. We hope *The Rules Handbook* was helpful in guiding you through all the stages of creating loving and long-lasting relationships. Remember, *The Rule*s work! As fulfilling as your career, children, grandchildren, girlfriends, charity work, and hobbies are, they're not quite the same as sharing your life with a romantic partner. Even if you've had a successful marriage, you might find that some days being a team player with your partner is hard to continue after you've been married a few years. And this is why we created a two-week reminder course of "the best of" daily reminders that will help remind you of how to use *The Rules* to empower your *Higher Self* in your everyday life and inspire you to stay on *The Rules* path. In addition to the following two-week reminder course, you can also use support groups (there are Facebook pages Rules Girls can join), dating coaches (either us or one of many women we have trained and certified in *The Rules*), as well as finding encouragement, helpful hints, and success stories on our Facebook and Instagram pages.

WEEK ONE
Reminders Before You
Jump Back into *The Rules*

Day 352: Leap of Faith
MONDAY

The Rules require a certain leap of faith. Against your better judgment and rational thinking, we're asking you to believe that letting men speak to you first and pulling back (playing hard to get) is going to make him want you more, not less, and that he's going to think that you're intriguing and busy, not rude. Naturally, you are filled with trepidation. You're afraid the strategy is going to backfire, that he'll think you're not interested and move on to someone else who shows a lot of interest. We get that you're afraid and risk-avoidant, but men aren't. In fact, they love high-speed car chases, bungee jumping, and bullfights (all the things women find terrifying), and they fall in love with women who are a little hard to get! So if you want to get the guy, don't worry and control so much—just play *The Rules* game!

Day 353: Excuses, but No Reason
TUESDAY

There's always an excuse to not date right now. Work is crazy, you're shopping for a new car, you're redoing your kitchen, your cat needs to go to the vet again, you started a vegetarian diet that may be hard to navigate at restaurants, yada yada. We've heard it all. The truth is, there is always going to be something. You don't have to date all day and night. We're talking about an hour here and there—three hours a week—of going out and checking your online messages. It doesn't have to be all-or-nothing or perfect. It just has to be now. If not now, when?

Day 354: Stop Fighting

WEDNESDAY

It's not *The Rules* but your resistance to *The Rules* that make them hard to do. Clients have told us that their first reaction to our book was "I'm not a 1950s housewife," or "This is crazy. I went to college; I should be able to do whatever I want," or "Why should I have to play games? If a guy asks me out on Friday for Saturday and I don't have plans, why not go?" Of course, after a difficult breakup or two, they're sold and want to know exactly what to do. The sooner you accept that love works best when the man pursues the woman, the sooner you won't struggle so much! When you want to break a rule, ask yourself, "Is this the woman I want to be, the woman who texts a guy to remind him I exist or shows up at his place unannounced demanding to know why he didn't answer my texts or calls?"

Day 355: Feminist and Feminine

THURSDAY

Thanks to feminism, most women are career-driven and financially independent. They own their own apartments, drive luxury cars, go on lavish vacations, and run half-marathons without a man and without thinking twice! The downside is they are more masculine and bring that masculine energy into their romantic relationships, and it doesn't work. *The Rules* answer is that you can be a feminist and feminine at the same time. We are! For the last twenty-five-plus years and without the assistance of a man, we have run our own corporation for relationship coaching, have written six books, and have appeared on every TV show, radio show, magazine, and newspaper, including *The Oprah Winfrey Show, Good Morning America, The Today Show, The Joan Rivers Show, People* magazine, and *The New York Times* as bestselling authors. We are go-getters with work, but try to be feminine at home with our husbands.

Day 356: Be Smart

FRIDAY

People who say that *The Rules* are a game and that there shouldn't be any intrigue in matters of the heart are living under a rock. Life is a game! You don't go on job interviews in pajamas or say how much you hate to work. You don't tell your mother-in-law that you married her son and not his family and that she shouldn't expect to see you that much. And you don't go on dates and talk about all your failed relationships. Women who think that they can say or do whatever they want are living in a dream world. There must be decorum, or there will be consequences. A woman with no filter went with her boyfriend to couples counseling and told the therapist that he was "a loser" for not making more money. He left the session and the relationship. She never heard from him again. Don't be naïve. Be smart and be a Rules Girl!

Day 357: Self-Examination

SATURDAY

If you don't examine all past and present relationships and look for self-sabotaging patterns (making the first move, being too available, only dating rich men who don't treat you well, etc.), how are you going to change? Knowledge is power! You have to own your mistakes and resolve to do better. Stop the blame game. It's your mother's fault for being critical, your father's fault for never being around, or your ex's fault for wasting your time and not committing. We disagree! There are no victims, only volunteers. Look at yourself objectively, not with shame or blame or self-hate, but to see what *Rules* you followed, what *Rules* you broke, and how or where you can do better!

Day 358: Self-Actualization

SUNDAY

While we have been talking a lot about the importance of dating and getting married to Mr. Right, we are big believers in being your own person and self-reliant. No matter how happily married you are, your husband can't be your everything. You still want to have your own life, meaningful work, friends, interests, hobbies, and passions, as long as you don't put them before him. Practice *The Rules for Marriage,* but also do *The Rules* on everyone so you are not hurt by people in general, whether it's your aloof sister-in-law, fair-weather friend, or nosy neighbor. *The Rules* prevent unnecessary pain and suffering. They are actually medicinal. It is common knowledge that people who are sick are told not to interact with difficult family or friends, as it would upset them and possibly weaken their immune system! *The Rules* (healthy boundaries) are a lifesaver!

WEEK TWO

Relationship Reminders

Day 359: Unprepared

MONDAY

Most women are sadly unprepared to be in a relationship or marriage. They are all about going to college, establishing their careers, paying off their student loans, and getting their own apartments. While all of the above is commendable, dating is, unfortunately, an afterthought. Dating today is also undisciplined, much like the Wild West: do whatever you feel like, and there are no *Rules*! Parents and professors are not teaching their daughters and students how to date or be married! So women are either in unhealthy relationships or miserably single because they're too aggressive or available with men. Or, they're married and thinking that it's all about outward appearances, the right restaurant reservations, apartment, or car, using your *Lower Self* instead of the inner work of navigating a loving and lasting relationship with your *Higher Self*. Alas, this handbook will tell you everything you need to know to get and stay married successfully!

Day 360: Focus on Self-Control

TUESDAY

You want results (the ring and marriage), but you also want to do whatever you feel like! Unfortunately, life doesn't work that way! *The Rules* are about self-control and confidence, two traits which are attractive to everyone, especially men! So stop focusing on what you can't do, like calling or texting him or asking him out, and focus on what you can do, like working, going to the gym, seeing friends, watching a movie, and doing charity work. Bonus: The discipline you apply to dating will hopefully translate into everything else you do . . . diet, exercise, alcohol consumption, bedtime, use of social media, time spent with friends, and so on. Your power is in self-control, not in pursuing men.

Day 361: Natural Cure

WEDNESDAY

The latest relationship buzz words are codependency, love addiction, toxicity, triggers, narcissism, dysfunction, post-traumatic stress disorder, shame, and reparenting the inner child. While addressing these issues with therapy or spirituality is, of course, desirable, we believe that doing *The Rules* naturally weeds out narcissists, time-wasters, and other Buyer Bewares. When you date with self-esteem, confidence, and boundaries, you effortlessly attract healthy partners people who want to be with you and marry you but who also want a reasonable amount of freedom and space, which is why we believe in leaving everyone alone!

Day 362: What If?

Don't try to out-think *The Rules*. Don't think, "If I do this, he'll think I'm playing games or that I'm rude, and he'll get angry and retaliate." First of all, no one can read your mind or prove you are doing *The Rules* or anything else; if he's angry, then he's a Buyer Beware who you don't want. But let's say a guy suspects or accidentally finds out that you are doing *The Rules* (maybe you forgot to hide your copy of this handbook in your apartment). If he likes you, he would be flattered! He would think it's cute that you're playing hard to get or being busy to get him. As for seeming rude, remember that guys have no problem ending a five-year relationship by text, so don't worry about taking five hours to text him back! Women often ask us "what-if" questions. "What if I write back short answers to an online guy and he complains that I'm cold?" The answer is he's not interested. He would not complain—he would just ask you out and talk to you on the date. "What if I refuse to meet him halfway and he says I'm inflexible?" Again, he doesn't like you because the right guy would drive long distances to be with you. Men drive for hours to football games and concerts without complaining. We remind clients that *The Rules* weed out men who are not that interested and are time-wasters!

Day 363: Healing
FRIDAY

Pain comes from attachment, wanting something or someone you can't have. You might feel heartbroken over an ex or feeling lonely in an existing relationship where you are not getting enough attention or your needs and wants (a ring and proposal) met. You might feel broken and in despair at ever finding the love of your life. This book is all about new beginnings and moving on from an ex or an unsatisfying relationship by following a formula. Don't make the first move with any man, and don't reach out to the person who is causing you pain. Love those who love you. Go where you are wanted. See who calls you. See who wants to be with you and go there. Look to the left and to the right, and that's who wants you. *The Rules* heal brokenness and pain!

Day 364: Look Back, but Don't Stare
SATURDAY

Whatever brought you to *The Rules Handbook*—a breakup, a divorce, unrequited love, a fantasy relationship, dating a married or unavailable man, disastrous dating app dates, a plethora of mistakes with men, or the complete absence of any love interest for years or decades—was a necessary bottom that was meant to be! No experience is for naught or ever wasted. Don't regret the past if it brought you to this place of truth, enlightenment, and realism about the way love works. That's why we had to write *The Rules* down to share with women the best way to date to marry and minimize man pain. You can and should examine the spots where you fell or missed the mark, but don't stare so hard or so much that you become paralyzed from moving on and squander the present and new opportunities. Don't look back so much that you're frozen.

Day 365: The Beginning of Hope

SUNDAY

The end of a relationship can feel like death. He won't commit. He broke your heart. You can't make him want you. You can't get him back. You are the definition of despair. You don't believe in love anymore. You've lost hope. You feel that love is for everyone but you. You may secretly hate and feel jealous of all your couple friends. You feel that life is unfair. You may feel that something is wrong with you, but not sure what to do or where to start. You don't give up.

You start by accepting that one door has closed in the Universe and another is going to open. You let go of the past and make a beginning in the present. You take one tiny action—you take a few selfies and join a dating app or dress up and go to a club or bar for an hour with a girlfriend. You circle the room and don't talk to any man first. When a man approaches you, *The Rules* have begun. If you're breathing, there's hope!

Of course, everyone is different and each situation is unique. If you have any questions or require a private consultation for your particular situation, please contact us at TheRulesBook.com.

We hope *The Rules Handbook* has given you all the dos and don'ts you need to meet your soulmate, along with the confidence, faith, and strength to move on and never give up!

ABOUT THE AUTHORS

Ellen Fein and Sherrie Schneider met in New York City circa 1990 when they were in their mid-twenties and became fast friends. Ellen had an accounting degree and was studying for her Masters in Social Work and Sherrie was a journalist. Both were career women who were told "you can do anything you want" in business and romance. They were never told that men and women are equal but different, that feminism didn't change biology, that men love a challenge, and that women need to "play hard to get" to get the guy.

Ellen got married first, having learned "The Rules," a set of dating dos and don'ts from a popular high school girl who told her that you can't chase guys the way you chase your career. "He has to notice you and ask you out." Ellen initially thought there were no "rules" or that rules were silly, but then used *The Rules* to catch her husband. She then shared these secrets with Sherrie, who was originally on the fence because she was more career-driven, but became sold as well.

Having personally experienced that *The Rules* work, they became passionate about helping other women use them to solve their dating problems. In addition, they shared a love for sitcoms (*I Love Lucy*, *Friends*, *Mad About You* and *Seinfeld*), Chinese food, swimming, and analyzing romantic TV shows and movies for *Rules* and non-*Rules* behavior.

In the late 1980s/early 1990s, they noticed a frightening epidemic or pandemic of sorts on TV and in real life: smart, attractive, nice women were knocking themselves out asking men out, planning dates, paying for drinks/dinner or going

Dutch, moving in, decorating men's apartments, and getting little or nothing in return, certainly not a proposal.

Single women were wasting time with the wrong men (Buyer Beware men, men they pursued and spoiled, and unavailable or married men) or breaking rules (calling too much, seeing men 24/7, and being codependent or controlling) with men who initially pursued them and getting hurt. It was like the Wild West with dating.

They felt this female aggressive behavior inevitably backfired and had to be stopped. They believed *The Rules* was not a "game" but a spiritual "game plan" to find one's soulmate. They matter-of-factly told women that the only way to know if a guy likes you is to "look to the left and look to the right and see who won't leave you alone, who's calling, who's asking you out—that's the guy who likes you!"

It was radical advice compared to the therapy-oriented books on the market telling women to "reach out first because he's probably busy with his new job; that's why you haven't heard from him." Ellen and Sherrie felt that women were being fed lies by well-meaning family, friends, fervent feminists, and so-called relationship experts and believed that *The Rules* was the real truth about dating!

The dynamic duo took calls morning, noon, and night and met weekly with friends and friends of friends at a Chinese restaurant on the Upper East Side, much like *Sex and the City* before *Sex and the City*. Every girl would bring her dating problem to the table and was told what to do or not to do.

"A bathing suit for your birthday after a year of dating? We don't care if it's from Bloomingdale's, it should be jewelry...Next!" Or, "He wants you to go on an overseas business trip with him for the third date? No way, don't be flattered. A week away should be your honeymoon!"

They were like secret sociologists at dinners, weddings, and other social events, determining who liked whom and whether a couple was meant to be or doomed. Everything was based on variations of how they met and "who spoke to whom first." Friends of friends of friends started calling with *Rules* questions.

But when these women went on actual dates, they became nervous and could barely remember anything, so they started writing important *Rules* on the palm of their hands, such as "End the Date First." At this point, Ellen was married with children and couldn't handle all the calls so she told Sherrie that they should write a *Rules* dating book like an instruction manual.

Sherrie became engaged soon after and was one of many *Rules* success stories, proving that the "playing hard to get" philosophy worked. The first *Rules* book was published in 1995 and became a #1 *New York Times* bestseller.

Ellen and Sherrie did the usual media tour, culminating in a trip to London to be on the *Richard and Judy* morning show (the equivalent of *Kelly and Ryan*). It was July 1, 1996, Princess Di's 35th birthday. Julia Carling, a TV presenter, announced that she was sending the bestseller to Princes Di and circled the chapter "Don't Date A Married Man," as it was rumored that Di was flirting with Julia's rugby player husband. The British tabloids ran the story and *Page Six* picked it up. Everyone wanted to know what book Princess Di was sent for her birthday!

Every TV show from *Oprah* to the *Today Show* and every newspaper and magazine contacted them. In fact, *People* magazine offered to make *The Rules* their cover story if Ellen and Sherrie gave them photos of their husbands and children. They said no because becoming famous didn't change their morals. They believed in protecting their family's privacy and still do.

Support groups sprung all over. Rules Girls met in their apartments or coffee shops and libraries in cities around the world to discuss the new "dating bible." Women wrote Ellen and Sherrie lengthy handwritten letters asking for specific solutions to their situations, so the coauthors became dating coaches as well, offering private phone and email consultations. They also ran seminars and courses training Rules Girls to become certified coaches, as well as how to become more confident and charming to counteract the badass movement that was becoming popular.

Becoming famous (they were parodied on *Saturday Night Live* and mentioned dozens of times on TV shows and sitcoms) didn't change their raison d'être. Ellen and Sherrie (or "Shellen," as fans like to call them) were still all about helping the single girl get and keep the guy. In fact, when they went back to London 10 years later to speak at The O2 venue, they ran back to their hotel room to do a radio show and call all 50 women who left messages about their dating dilemmas on their answering machine.

Ellen and Sherrie remain best friends and business partners. They speak several times a day to discuss clients' situations and dating trends/celebrity relationships that they can use to teach *The Rules* in their courses and on social media. They frequently post success stories on Facebook and Instagram to show women that *The Rules* still work and to counteract all the bad dating advice out there ("It's 2023...of course you can ask a man out and follow him on Instagram first"). Some women simply refuse to accept that men and women are different. They want to believe the fantasy that they can do anything they want with the opposite sex and succeed. If only that were true!

Ellen and Sherrie are frequently invited to their clients' weddings, but they decline because they're like Spanx, not to be seen or heard. They still get letters and fan mail from clients thanking them "for their wonderful husbands and children" or "for ending things with a married man" or "getting over an ex." Generation X and millennials call, email, and text with questions about dating with Facebook, Instagram, and other social media (no, friending you on Facebook is not a date or relationship).

Today, Ellen and Sherrie are both married with children and have helped millions of women around the world do *The Rules*. Ellen and Sherrie continue to help women with confidence and self-esteem, dressing for men (in-person and online makeovers, including clothes, makeup, and hair), dating and marriage, and *The Rules Handbook* (more dating and marriage rules plus rules for friends, family, and business associates). They continue to be passionate about their "playing hard to get" mission!

They have been approached by producers to do a reality show, and Paramount Pictures optioned the movie rights. Stay tuned!